Light of My Darkness

Carolyn Reese

PublishAmerica
Baltimore

© 2003 by Carolyn Reese.
All rights reserved. No part of this book may be reproduced in any form without written permission from the publishers, except by a reviewer who may quote brief passages in a review to be printed in a newspaper or magazine.

First printing

ISBN: 1-59286-738-3
PUBLISHED BY PUBLISHAMERICA BOOK PUBLISHERS
www.publishamerica.com
Baltimore

Printed in the United States of America

*For all who are
impacted by mental illness
and need hope
and encouragement.*

Acknowledgements

Special thanks go to Karan Kummer for her editorial expertise that was vital to this work. Her personal sensitivity and challenge to write from the heart positively affected my writing.

I am forever indebted to Rita Walker, Joyce Nalley, Dana Breitweiser, Diane Dow, Teresa White, John D'Arezzo, Carolyn Turk and Kim Riggan who had a part in my healing by their unconditional love and willingness to speak the truth. Their faith and presence solidified my determination to complete this book.

Thank you Sue McElroy for never doubting that I could write a book. Your faithfulness and honesty have upheld me every step of the way. You have spurred me on through some hard times in my life and your Godly wisdom and insight is sprinkled throughout my writing.

My life has been blessed by everyone who read the unfinished manuscript. Your words of praise and correction were invaluable.

I want to acknowledge my mother and father who I now know love me and believe in me.

My sisters and brother and their families are a constant source of strength and pleasure.

I have told my story especially for my children and grandchild so that they may learn of the love, mercy and unending goodness of our

Heavenly Father. May the life I live daily before them repeat clearly all that is said in this book.

Most of all, thank you God. You are my Everything.

Table of Contents

Chapter One...............11
The Delusion
Fear becomes reality

Chapter Two...............15
Sweet Sixteen and Wanting To Die
A personal account of sickness

Chapter Three...............27
We Are What We Think.
Thoughts must be chosen carefully.

Chapter Four...............39
I Don't Need A Therapist!
Our necessity: the conduit to God

Chapter Five...............47
I Can't Help It! This Is the Way I Was Made.
To change or stay the same is the decision of a lifetime.

Chapter Six...............53
Me Forgive? Never!
Forgiveness is a must for emotional health.

Chapter Seven...............59
Trying to be Perfect Is Mistake #1.
Measuring up silences uniqueness.

Chapter Eight...............67
Pay Attention to Me! I'm Sick!
Sickness has many rewards.

Chapter Nine...............75
I Need Somebody – Anybody! – To Love.
Love: we'll give up everything to find it.

Chapter Ten...............81
There's No Such Thing As Hopeless.
Never give up. I say again, never give up.

Chapter Eleven...............93
I'm Lonely, But Don't Ask Me To Do Anything About It.
Those incognito ogres: isolation and withdrawal

Chapter Twelve...............99
One Last Try
Satan fights dirty and will hit below the belt.

Chapter Thirteen...............103
But If I'm Not Healed, Something Is Wrong.
Can this too be healing?

Chapter Fourteen...............111
How Great Are Your Mercies Toward Us!
The gift of two dreams

Chapter Fifteen...............117
I'm in Control. I Can Handle This by Myself.
Only God is self-sufficient.

Chapter Sixteen...............123
Losing It All Again
God's plans are the best.

Chapter Seventeen...............135
Learning to Cope is What It's All About.
More strategies for creating hope, health and happiness

Chapter One
The Delusion
Fear becomes reality

    I was sixteen. I stood on the overpass looking down on the interstate. The voices snarled, "You worthless scum. No one can stand you. You can't do anything right. Jump off the bridge. Go on. Kill yourself. No one cares about you. Do it! Go on, do it!"
    Then I believed the voices more than anyone and later in life as a wife and mother, they were more important than my children and husband. They were stronger than sleeping pills and pleas to God to stop them. My thoughts were challenged and debated by them. As an impotent bystander, I readily accepted their logic and reasoning. When I argued, the voices united their efforts and confusion and defeat quickly overtook me. These other "persons" established my truth and were my constant companions.
    In my thirties and forties, they tortured me with a hideous fear that threatened to destroy me and all that I loved. I was alone in my mind for the voices had convinced me that help was futile. The few friends in whom I confided certainly offered assistance and truth. But this only revealed their ineptness in comprehending the reality of what I saw as my unique situation. Speedy rebuttals, on my part, indicated my annoyance and obsession with the details of my thoughts. I believed that others lacked my spiritual knowledge and depth of understanding. I maintained my enlightenment surpassed everyone's comprehension. The voices declared peace impossible. Therefore, for me, it was so.

The fear began with a delusion. I was asked to leave my family for Jesus. The voice that spoke was kind and soft, so I thought it had to be Jesus. I agonized over the thought, picturing in my mind how my children and others would feel betrayed and reject me. They would not understand what I was doing. But I decided to leave everyone for Jesus.

In the next scene, I saw myself walking down the street as Jesus, with a few converts following behind. My aloneness was heavy from the knowledge that no one shared the vision of my mission on earth or knew the depth of my profound calling. The voice asked if I was willing to endure emotional separation from all mankind and accept this irrevocable and total claim on my life. Again, I answered that I would.

The next question involved my willingness to die on the cross. The torment was nauseating and sweat covered my body. My breathing became quick and shallow as if physically wrestling with the thought. Each situation that led up to Jesus' death, I imagined myself experiencing. Standing before Pilate. Being ridiculed and whipped by the soldiers. The crown of thorns piercing my head. The weight of the cross pushing me to the ground. I assumed I could feel the pain of the nails being hammered in my hands and feet. After what seemed a long, long time, I answered yes; I would be willing to die just as Jesus had done.

Instantly, the kind voice changed to an evil rasping, "Then you will be my Antichrist!" I started screaming, "No! No! This cannot be! No! No!" again and again, for I knew Satan had tricked me. I fell down into a dark tunnel-like hole still shrieking wildly. I yelled in panic and terror over and over and louder and louder. I cried out to God to save me and help me. My fingers clawed furiously into the sides of the dirt tunnel causing clods and pebbles to fly off as I tried to pull myself up. Still breathlessly pleading with God, I slowly came out of the tunnel and felt safe and rescued. Then I woke up; believing the nightmare was over.

It was not long before I "knew" I was the Antichrist. The delusion was now my reality. Alone, I faced the most horribly conceived scheme of destruction.

Because of my superior wisdom, I would be in demand as a speaker. People would come to me, as they did to Solomon, seeking my advice. My fame would spread worldwide as my knowledge solved all problems.

Quickly, I'd be elevated to ranks of high regard. Eventually, I would become the respected and honored world leader. I would believe that I was in God's will, for that was my desire. Being one of God's chosen children made me morally and spiritually superior to all believers.

Then it would happen. I would become the evil person I really was. God had tricked me - - I was Satan's child.

The shock was horrifying, for there was no way to stop the circumstances that would lead to being the Antichrist. I could only delay them by fighting the inevitable and staying strong. It was gut-wrenching agony of mind and body. I could not lose my mind, but I didn't have the strength to sustain my fight forever. Each face-to-face conflict with the evil weakened me and my time of horror grew a little closer. I would finally lose control and be completely lost. Then all hope would be gone. I knew I would be the center of prophesied events as the Bible declared.

One time I was too tired and defeated to resist the warfare anymore and I resigned myself to being the Antichrist. If this was what God had planned for me, then I wanted to do His will, even if it meant this. I just wanted to please Him. My twisted mind found a loophole to slip out of the web of entrapment. I was euphoric, delighting myself in the clever escape; for I knew God had arranged it for me. Then, as deftly and swiftly as the deliverance occurred, I was caught up in the former maze of fear and confusion. The Antichrist fear ruled my life for fifteen years.

Affirmations From God's Word

Consider my affliction and deliver me, for I do not forget Your law. Plead my cause and redeem me; revive me and give me life according to Your word. *Psalm 119:153,154*

We do not know what to do, but our eyes are upon You. For the battle is not yours, but God's. *II Chronicles 20:12,15*

We were so utterly and unbearably weighed down and crushed that we despaired even of life itself…but that was to keep us from trusting in and depending on ourselves instead of on God Who raises the dead. *II Corinthians 1:8,9*

In the shadow of Your wings will I take refuge and be confident until calamities and destructive storms are passed. *Psalm 57:1*

Reflective Reassurance

In times like these, I had no idea of how to help myself. Everything in my life seemed out of my control and beyond hope and help. I rarely told doctors or therapists anything about this fear. It was too disturbing.

One time I wrote the word Antichrist on a piece of paper for a therapist. I dared not say the word. As I spoke in very general and evasive terms, my body curled into a fetal position while sitting in a chair.

These verses tell us that this kind of battle is God's to fight for us. Our job is to take refuge in Him. Like a hen faithfully covers her chicks when danger is near, so God can be depended on to protect and deliver us. It can be so very hard to trust. But God will honor even our smallest efforts to trust Him in our afflictions.

Chapter 2
Sweet Sixteen and Wanting To Die
A personal account of sickness

As a sixteen-year-old in the State Hospital, I expressed my longing for unconditional love and the need to feel special in some extreme ways. My behavior corresponded to how well my needs were being met. No matter what my behavior was, it was my way of trying to fulfill my needs or denying that I had any. I was just like everyone else in this respect. I only varied in my ability to fulfill my needs.

We have two basic psychological needs: the need to love and be loved and the need to feel we are worthwhile to ourselves and to others. If our family cannot or will not give them, we look to other people to be our "family." Possessiveness of others may become a way of getting and trying to keep what we need. Extreme jealousy may shout out our past abandonment and be our way of not letting it ever happen again. Finding acceptance in a peer group or in a gang can be a way to get love, security and a feeling of value and worth. Our clothes and hairstyle can get us noticed. Doing daring and dangerous things may help us feel powerful and get attention. Our own hurt, pain and rejection seem to justify hurting other people.

All of life's problems are rooted in the same basic longings and needs. When we try to meet needs through illegitimate ways, we end up unbalanced and in pain. The harder and longer we persist in the wrong way, the more extreme and bizarre behaviors can become. Schizophrenia is an extreme exaggeration of the same things everyone deals with in life.

Children are good at letting us know their needs by their behavior.

Words do not come as easy for them as for most adults, so they act out their needs in ways that speak loud and clear. Many adults that lack social and emotional skills engage also in acting out behaviors that speak volumes to the observant and caring person. If we don't talk it out, we will act it out.

All the silent pent-up fears came rushing headlong into my consciousness with my brother's birth. I was the oldest of three girls and my brother was the baby. I lived with the knowledge that I was a disappointment because I was a girl. I was not wanted and I knew each of us girls represented efforts to get a boy. I heard this being talked about to guests while seated around the kitchen table. My name should have been Thomas William.

My parents' prayers were answered with my brother's birth when I was ten years old. It was obvious that nothing pleased them more than their son. Our family now revolved around him in what seemed like worship of the long awaited child.

I was convinced that I was no longer loved or special. I was now a nobody—an unwanted child. There was no place for me because their now-realized dream had come true. My position in the family had always been a precarious one. There had been a place for me only as long as there was no son. I learned from the birth of my brother that a person's love is strictly conditional and can change at any moment. And I learned that I was an unlovable person.

I now despised being a girl. All I wanted was to be a boy. Desperately I attempted to be the boy they wanted. My hair was cut short and parted on the side. Then I pinned back the sides to look like a boy's haircut. I wore long sleeve flannel shirts and jeans. My love became softball, and like my Dad, I became an avid Cardinal baseball fan. I talked about my desire to be the first woman professional baseball player on an all men's team. I determined to make good grades. Hours were spent alone in study. Reports were researched and rewritten to get them just right. My good grades were efforts to get noticed and fill the emptiness with busyness. Much time was devoted to playing with and entertaining my brother. I believed that doing all these things would make me loved and special again.

From my perspective, nothing worked. It seemed that no one noticed or cared what I was doing. No one came to my softball games. My sisters and I had to find our own transportation to and from our games. No emphasis was put on scholarship or high grades. Taking care of my brother was just expected behavior.

I watched my brother receive preferential treatment in ways us girls never enjoyed. I watched my parents' eyes dance at everything he did, like he was someone more than human. I loved my baby brother, but hated my parents.

The seating arrangement in the '62 Ford station wagon said a lot. There were eight people in the car and my brother was up front between my Mom and Dad. The cool air blew directly on him. My younger sister and I sat in the second seat and my youngest sister sat in the third seat. No air reached her and the sun bore down on her back much of the trip. My aunt and uncle each sat in the front and middle seat. This seating arrangement remained the same all the way to California and back.

My brother stared at the small pile of broccoli on his plate. "You have to eat your broccoli before you can get up," my mother stated again. My brother continued to whine and argue. Then Dad came in the room. He placed his hands on my brother's shoulders.

"Let him get up. He can't help it if he doesn't like broccoli." I watched as my brother was set free to do whatever he pleased. I recalled clearly the times my sisters and I had to sit there until every piece was gone.

According to Anthony Storr in *Human Aggression*: "Aggression that has remained unexpressed and not come to terms with will be: 1) repressed and turned inward against the self; 2) disowned and attributed to others; 3) expressed in explosive, childish forms."

In my childhood, as I continued to entertain and feed anger, fear and hate to the exclusion of healthy traits, my nonpsychotic symptoms grew deeper and darker. At the end of sixth grade, my class voted to go to the fair as a graduation celebration. The kids excitedly made plans for a fun-filled day. I worked on a plan to not go. I could not admit my unwillingness to freely laugh, scream on a ride or talk with classmates. I told the teacher that my mother wanted me to stay home and watch my baby brother. This story reflected negatively on my mother and that pleased me greatly.

Most people who develop schizophrenia display some signs and symptoms before the actual onset of the disease. This is often referred to as the "something is not right" phase. The average length of this period is two years. It can range from six months to five or more years.

It is not uncommon for some kind of stressor or change in the environment to come before the appearance of the illness. The person's ability to deal with this shift in circumstances may be limited or nonexistent. Undeveloped social skills, the lack of an available support system of family and friends and the inability to express feelings in appropriate and healthy ways all contribute to not having what it takes to adjust to adverse conditions in one's life.

In seventh and eighth grade, I went to a parochial school. I rarely talked to anyone. On my thirteenth birthday, the girls in my class went together and bought me a corsage. The girl that gave it to me said that they wanted to be my friends. The gift was deeply appreciated, but nothing changed. Still alone and withdrawn, I occasionally wrote letters to the pastor and principal. I would lay them on their desks when no one was around. It was my way of letting someone know I was in emotional trouble. They never spoke to me about the letters. I longed for them to say something to me about them and to help me. It was another example to me that no one cared or noticed me.

From the age of ten, when my brother was born, to sixteen, my world shifted radically. My mind exhausted itself with hate, disgust, fear and feelings of worthlessness. They ruled my life and my spirit. I told no one what I was feeling, because it was too horrible to tell. No one hated their mother. No one wanted to kill their mother. This was something unthinkable and unspeakable. I saw my mother as the only perfect mother; and yet now I hated her and wanted to kill her. How I despised myself! On the outside, I tried to pretend all was well. It seemed I only heard and saw evidences of me not being loved. Every situation and conversation proved that fact. I saw myself as an afterthought and the black sheep of the family. My perception of what was happening became my reality.

Rage toward my mother welled up inside of me. Obsessively, my only thoughts were of hatred for her. She abandoned me. She was the one person who could have rescued me, but didn't. Therefore, I blamed her. While my Mom stood at the stove cooking, I picked up a butcher knife from the kitchen table. Without my Mother's knowledge, I held it to her back while I contemplated whether to hurt her. When she began to turn around, I laid it back on the table in quiet resignation. I hated my mother for not being there for me. I hated myself because I hated her.

There was an overpass about a mile from our house. Walking or riding my bike there alone to think became a pattern. I wanted to jump off the overpass and became aware that I could no longer resist the desire. After a youth meeting at church, I asked the leaders if I could go to their house and talk. I told them what I was thinking about doing and that I didn't care what they did with me. I just knew I couldn't stop myself any longer. They called someone right then and later took me home.

My Dad did not want me to go to a hospital. The shame of mental illness was too great. He said he would work with me to solve my problems. My mother had a difficult time persuading him otherwise. At age sixteen, in April of my sophomore year of high school, I entered Barnes Hospital where I remained for three months. Then I went to the Youth Center at the state hospital for one year.

Self-mutilation, banging my head on the wall and attempted suicide were ways I cried out for understanding as a sixteen year old in the hospital. I had never expressed my feelings before to anyone. I denied that I had any. But as I watched other kids in the hospital act out their pain, I realized this was a safe place. I hit my head on the wall because I was no good. I knew I was not loved. I felt ugly, angry and sad. I hated myself and knew everything I attempted was no good. Because my self-esteem was nil, I perceived most things as hurtful and critical. I was constantly thinking about everything that was wrong with me, so I expected others to find fault with me too. Any kind of a mistake shouted out that I was bad and worthless. Feeling unloved was internalized as "I am no good," not even good enough for my own Mom and Dad to love me or care about me.

At the Youth Center, many expressions of my self-hatred emerged. I was in line at the cafeteria for lunch, when an irresistible urge to hurt myself came over me. When picking up my silverware, I concealed a fork by placing the tines in my palm with the handle against the inside of my arm. The girl behind me saw what I was doing. As I began to walk and then run toward the bathrooms, she ran after me, jumped on my back and knocked me to the floor. She attempted to get the fork from my hand, but I struggled loose and went into the boy's bathroom. I was able to place one foot against the door and the other against an inside wall to keep the door from opening. Ignoring their calls to me from outside the door, I began scratching and cutting my arm with the fork. When I felt finished, I opened the door and was taken back upstairs.

One day, boxes of donated clothes arrived. We could go through them and pick out anything we wanted. Excitement welled inside me for now I could find a belt. Looking through the clothes, I paid strict attention to only them. When I found the one I wanted, I rolled it tightly in a coil and put it in the palm of my hand. Trying not to be noticed and with my heart pounding, I walked back to my room and hid the belt. Plans had already been made to end my life.

My room at the center was directly across from the nurse's station. I had been told to leave the door open at all times. That evening, while everyone was watching TV or playing games, I slipped into my room without being noticed. Quietly, my hands turned the doorknob to shut the door. It was dark except for the soft glow of the streetlights below. I got the belt and put it around my neck while standing on a chair. The end of the belt was in the top of the closed door of a freestanding metal closet. As I was lowering myself from the chair, the nurses looked in through a small window and rushed in with scissors to cut me down.

One weekend while on leave from the center, I went downstairs to my Dad's workroom. I hunted through his drawers and on his workbench until I found a sharp piece of metal that would fit in the hem of my coat. When back at the center, I used it to scratch and cut my arm again. I also used combs to hurt myself as I rubbed them harshly back and forth on the back of my hand and fingers. A sharp pencil produced a puncture wound on my arm. My left arm was bandaged from just below the shoulder to the end of my fingers. Banging my head on the walls was a daily occurrence.

After trying to hang myself, I was not left alone. An aide stayed beside me and even watched me shower. She told me she would not talk to me anymore if I continued to hurt myself and try to take my life. My bed was pulled in front of the open door of my room to be in full view while I slept. That night a terrible nightmare woke me. I was screaming, "She doesn't love me anymore!" "She doesn't love me anymore!" The aides came rushing in to find me crying and shaking in fear. I told them of my conversation with the aide earlier in the day and that she did not love me anymore. The next afternoon this aide assured me that she did not mean what she had threatened to do.

The usual routine after I banged my head on the wall or hurt myself was to be given a shot and then be strapped to my bed. One aide began telling me she didn't believe I needed shots and restraints anymore. Instead, she laid her small body on top of mine and held my hands down on the bed. She would talk to me in soothing tones to calm and distract. Her special attention made a deep impression. I began to feel cared about and special. The length of time that she held me became less and less and eventually I did not bang my head any more or need restraints.

At semester in January, I was enrolled in a high school within walking distance of the Youth Center. The halls were crowded with kids going in every direction. I felt lost and alone and unready for this step. After the first day, I said I could not do it, and my high school attendance was dropped.

At the Youth Center, I attended a history and sewing class. There were about six students in sewing and three in history. There was no homework or tests. On the last day of the history class, the male teacher asked me to stay after the others had left. He told me what a pleasure I was to have in his class and then he kissed me. It was a passionate, lengthy kiss. I was shocked and unable to say anything. I left confused and unable to explain what had happened. Looking back on it as an adult, I could only surmise that my psychiatrist had talked to him about doing this to help me feel good about myself.

Before school started again in the fall, I was discharged. My psychiatrist stated that he knew my reason for being hospitalized had not been resolved, but he did not want me to miss another year of school. In response to not wanting to leave him, I began getting out a picture of myself from my purse with hair fixed like a boy to help him understand. I told him that I once wanted to be a boy. He quickly dismissed my first attempt at opening up by saying, "Oh, I'm sure it was just the usual tomboy stage all girls go through at that age." I put the picture away and never spoke of this again to him.

During this time and into middle age, I would become strongly attracted to anyone who cared or gave me approval. Typical behaviors included pleasing, giving gifts, hanging on every word, and saying what I thought they wanted to hear. I needed someone to love me. If I wasn't this person's dearest, all-consuming friend for all-time, I knew I was rejected again as unlovable. If this person did not speak glowingly of me in all areas of my life, then I knew I had to try harder to please and impress. Like a microscope looking for the smallest evidences of detail, I was super-sensitive to rejection. My radar zeroed in on anything remotely suggesting possible rejection or pulling away.

The psychiatrist at the Youth Center payed special attention to me. He took me to eat out, visit museums and other attractions. Sometimes we just went for a drive. He said he wanted me to experience and be knowledgeable of life. He said he wanted me to know that I was attractive and to think well of myself. His attentions continued on Saturdays for several months after I was discharged. I would ride the bus into the city to his office. There I would wait for him to finish with his last patient around noon. Then the rest of the day and evening was our time together.

One afternoon we stopped on a deserted country road. He put his hand in my blouse. I wanted to run across the open fields and escape. How could a married man be doing this to me? When he asked how I felt and I told him, he said he would run after me. I never mentioned that his behavior confused me. I didn't want him to stop loving me.

Another time, we sat parked under an arch at night. He explained the design and the difficulty in constructing such a shape. He was my doctor, my teacher, my first love. I listened carefully to all that he said and would do anything he asked to keep from being rejected again. He asked me to touch him. Dutifully, I felt through his slacks and again was flushed with agitating questions and guilt.

Eventually, as different sexual situations arose, the questions became clouded by infatuation on my part. I had finally found someone who loved me for who I was. His love was unconditional and did not depend on what I did. I thought about him all the time and knew there was no one else like him in the whole world. I wrote out the words to Elvis Presley's hit song, "I Can't Help Falling in Love With You" and gave them to him. They expressed my devotion and all that I wanted to say to him. I wanted to marry him although he was old enough to be my grandfather. If I became twenty-six and was still unmarried, he said we would marry.

One night he stopped at a hotel and bought me a gift. Knowing that I collected woodcarvings, he purchased a beautifully hewn young boy. I made the statement that we should get a room and spend the night. He would not for fear of losing his license. His attentions continued to be in his car.

Since transporting a minor across state lines was prohibited, he appeared sad that he could not take me to his home. He spoke of things in his home that he wanted me to see and enjoy. He showed me a picture of his wife and explained that she was a teacher.

We crossed the Mississippi River bridge at different times in our excursions. The bridge was narrow and the water seemed only a step away. Wanting to die rushed all over me as I reached for the door handle that would fling me out and into the deep water. It seemed the doctor's arm was always extended to grab me each time I moved toward the door. It was reassuring to know that someone cared enough to stop me.

It took me nearly thirty-five years to realize this man did not love me. Letting go meant I would experience rejection once again. God didn't ask me to loosen my grip on the belief that this man truly loved me until He knew I was ready. He has lovingly strengthened me through the years for what I thought I could never do. God brought it to my rapt attention about a year ago. A friend boldly declared I was wrong and said this man had sexually molested me. I did my usual routine of refusing to listen and continuing to defend his behavior. But this time I entertained the possibility that she was right. I pictured this same behavior played out in one of my students' lives or a staff therapist where I worked doing such a thing. I acknowledged it would be very wrong for them. A few months later, the relationship with the psychiatrist came up again with a different friend. This time I admitted his wrongdoing because I was ready. The emotional pain remained minimal. God knew how long it would take before I could handle the truth. He did not rush me. He never expects us to do something He has not prepared us to do.

Affirmations From God's Word

A calm and undisturbed mind and heart are the life and health of the body, but envy, jealousy, and wrath are like rottenness to the bones. *Proverbs 14:30*

Behold, it was for my peace that I had intense bitterness; but You have loved back my life from the pit of corruption and nothingness, for You have cast all my sins behind Your back. *Isaiah 38:17*

The Lord does not delay and is not tardy or slow about what He promises, according to some people's conception of slowness, but He is long suffering (extraordinarily patient) toward you, not desiring that any should perish, but that all should return to repentance. *II Peter 3:9*

Reflective Reassurance

We want hard things over with quickly. God has a lot more in mind than just relieving our pain. He has to refashion us in many different ways. When sin came into the world, it grotesquely altered our likeness to our heavenly Father. God's perfect design for us had coffee stains and scribbles all over it. God works faithfully to redo His plan for us that He began before the beginning of time. He waits until we are ready, never forcing Himself on us.

"His Thoughts Toward Me"
by Marie Chapian

I am the One who gives you new life,
who yanks sin and hatred from you.
Would you accuse Me of sending you
that which I have freed you from?

Chapter Three
We Are What We Think
Thoughts must be chosen carefully

When I consider the strong, unexpressed, emotions raging inside of me six years prior to the development of my symptoms at age sixteen, I must agree with Lord Byron when he said, "Hatred is the madness of the heart." Anger, hate, revenge, self-loathing and guilt were my masters. As the years passed, they became powerfully entrenched and governed my perspective on everyone and everything. Even into middle age, a spirit of criticalness and perfectionism prevented me from seeing any good in my parents. Anger skewed my perception of everything about them. I had no compassion for them and could not assume the best about them. They had it coming to them for not meeting my needs as a child and not measuring up to my unrealistic expectations.

After graduating from high school, I went to a junior college where I met my husband. I married at age twenty and remained symptom free until my early thirties when a situation in my marriage brought the disease of paranoid schizophrenia back to life. I believed I was losing the love of my husband. I was willing to do whatever it took to keep him loving me, even if that meant going against what I believed was morally right. I followed my husband's wishes, but I could not reconcile the wrong I had done. This created the crisis that triggered the return of the schizophrenia. After several years, my husband grew weary of the disease and divorced me. Intense anger and hatred now included my ex-husband as well as my Mom and

Dad. The loss of love a second time was almost too much to bear.

When the schizophrenia returned, it was compounded by depression. All the childhood thoughts of self-hatred and worthlessness came back in double force. I was overcome by the strength of the blow. Months were spent in bed with the covers pulled tight. My mind reeled in shock, unable to concentrate or make any decision. Numbness enveloped my spirit as I slipped deeper and deeper into confusion and despair.

I was unable to function as a wife or mother. For hours, I would stare into space not knowing what was happening around me. Being interrupted or distracted was not appreciated. It could be said that thoughts were my companion and I enjoyed being alone with them. There were times I didn't want to sleep because my thoughts would be interrupted and I would not be able to pick up where I had left off. Irritability welled up in me and I resisted people that encouraged meaningful activities. I liked where I was and what I was doing. Continual days and nights were spent in my own world. And that was fine with me.

Thoughts ran free in my mind with no supervision. I listened and "watched" as they fed off each other, multiplying wildly and crazily. I did not know I could control them or examine them. I thought them; therefore, they were real and unstoppable. I was quickly becoming the sum total of my thoughts. I would lie awake at night for hours, while riveted to constant bombardment of thoughts. They went in countless directions; but always ended in fear and confusion. Losing sleep only weakened my defenses further.

Unhealthiness is a process built on mistaken beliefs that are held strongly over time. I developed a mind-set that validated everything I believed. Error was built on top of error to entrap me further. I lived out my thoughts and beliefs and became twisted mentally, physically and spiritually. My body responded to stimuli that my mind said was present and real. I was centered on self-pity and the people I perceived had hurt me. I was no longer the same person on the outside or inside since the schizophrenia began the second time.

My negative thoughts eventually became habits and over time

created my personality. Thoughts took me to places no one understood. When self-absorption became extreme, it was impossible to make sense. Others could no longer relate or show empathy. People did not interest me. They were a bother. Compassion and caring for others were gone. I sounded, looked and acted crazy. I didn't understand what had happened or how I had gotten so lost inside myself. And I sure didn't know the way out.

My young daughter, aged seven, sat in the middle of her bed pounding it and screaming, "Tell me what is wrong! I've got to know what is wrong!" I did not have a clue of what to tell her. I simply answered again and again, "I don't know."

Many different medications were started and then stopped by my psychiatrist. It took several months to find the one that brought relief. I stayed with it for twenty years; and the longer I was on it, the more I improved. The dosage now remains at a minimum unless I have trouble. Then it will be increased for awhile until I am stable again.

Modern drugs for schizophrenia and depression affect the brain chemistry. Key to many of these drugs are the chemicals dopamine and serotonin. They are neurotransmitters and carry messages between the nerve cells. They occur naturally in the brain but are out of balance in schizophrenia and depression. Drugs that are effective in schizophrenia block dopamine. Researchers suspect that an excess of dopamine results from the progression of the disease. Why the dopamine is altered is unknown. Possible theories include a genetic defect, stress, or a virus. Serotonin is known to affect mood. Low serotonin levels are associated with irritability and sadness.

The importance of medication in schizophrenia and depression cannot be denied. The Old Testament has always linked mental processes and health. "A merry heart doeth good like a medicine," says the Book of Proverbs, "but a broken spirit drieth the bones."

Getting good sleep was such a problem. My therapist suggested I get sleeping pills from my family doctor. This time I had gone eight days without sleep. The doctor available had never seen me before. He began by giving a stern talk on the dangers of sleeping aids and why they should be avoided. Then he said to tell him why I needed sleeping pills. How could I ever explain all my problems to him? It was overwhelming and too hard to tell. I told him to call my therapist at the clinic. He insisted on hearing the reason from me. After telling him three times to speak to the therapist, I ran out of the office crying.

Staying in my own world was an effective way of escaping pain and responsibility for problems. The world and the people in it were separated from me. Life was too hard. I felt scared, alone, angry and terribly confused. My busy thought-life became a comfortable and calming antidote for the harsh reality of the sin in my marriage that I knew was unforgivable.

Inside my mind, I could be in control and be the capable and strong person I wanted so desperately to be. I lacked the knowledge, skills, past experiences and strong support system that instills and teaches the courage and determination to deal with real life. Therefore, I made my own reality in my mind. By escaping, I found a way to gain mastery over my environment.

My body was hanging onto the harmful thoughts also and followed suit with negative changes and responses. My moods changed from moment to moment depending on circumstances and people. Anxiety, fear, withdrawal and suspicion colored my personality a strange and foreboding hue. Major depression impacted my health, gait, speech and affect. And the delicate balance of body and brain chemistry reflected upheaval and disarray. Positive influences we take for granted such as sunshine, fresh air, social contacts, balanced diet, laughter, fun and exercise were replaced with seclusion, drawn blinds, weight loss, and severe fatigue.

Schizophrenia and depression weighed heavily on my ability to think and respond. The despair was so great that there was no energy to answer or move freely. Hopelessness squelched even the smallest effort to communicate. It took all my strength just to sit up and move when required. A response was not worth the exertion. I heard everything said to me and about me, but I rarely spoke. Words wouldn't make any difference. No one understood or really cared anyway.

For many schizophrenics, few relatives or friends dare to venture in to help when behavior becomes so twisted and strange. They have no idea of what to do and become understandably frustrated by the seemingly endless demands of emotional and mental unhealthiness. My friends stayed close, but my family never knew how serious my problems were since they were all out of state and did not visit often.

I had to begin the rigorous process of slowing my thoughts down to get out of this lethal and inaccessible pit of disease that I fashioned with my own thoughts. I needed to be aware of patterns and pitfalls that sucked me unknowingly into the bizarre. Each night an intense fight began as I tried to focus on just one or two thoughts and then go to sleep. In the wee hours of the morning, I would find myself snapping to just enough to realize I had been thinking once again for hours. Living in my own world was now all I could do. The freedom to choose was gone.

I needed to become consumed and centered in on someone else, namely, God. He was the only One who knew where I was and how I got there. He could get me out and stand me on solid ground. Only He had the power to change me and make me useful once again. I remembered the phrase, "Just when you think God is all you have, you find He is all you need," and it applied to me.

It is evident that these adverse attitudes of hate, anger and fear are not God-inspired. Virtually every book of the Bible exhorts us to refrain from them. God warns us against them because they are physical expressions of spiritual problems.

How could a spiritual problem ever apply to me? I knew I loved God and that my heart was turned toward Him. I felt angry and misunderstood whenever this was mentioned. In later years, I came to understand that many choices I made were rooted in sin that had been passed from one generation of my family to the next. The burning desire to break the cycle in my own life and the lives of my children spurred me on to make many difficult changes.

I was unable to have an intimate and personal relationship with a loving, forgiving, trustworthy God when I was neck deep in hate, bitterness and fear. An angry, bitter person will not let another person get close and love them. My self-centeredness and self-pity excluded even God, for I felt unworthy of anything good and I could not trust even God. These were bright, red, warning flags that something was wrong. I could not progress until the signals of caution were heeded and I was convinced God was my Perfect Helper.

I learned that God longed to honor my efforts in overcoming the sin in my life. When I asked for God's forgiveness and His help, my hate began turning to love and my bitterness to compassion. I began to see evidences of my sufferings turning into gladness and having meaning.

As I continued to grow through Christian radio, friends, reading and going to church regularly, I learned some important things about my mind and it's thoughts.

My mind is my battlefield. All of my struggles and triumphs are fought and won there. My thoughts create who I become, for every thought has physical expression. What I pay attention to increases in me until it is what I attain. The way I think determines the way I respond.

It is like a garden. If I want something to grow, I must sow it, care for it and spend time nurturing its growth. The same process is true for the thoughts I allow to enter my mind and be entertained, cherished and developed. Whatever I sow in my mind now, I will reap in my behavior later. This is the cornerstone that supports the foundation for my mental wellness or my mental illness.

Every thought must be taken captive. I must guard the thoughts that enter my mind. It is essential to screen them and spend time only with the ones that build up and encourage positive and helpful action. Thoughts that run amuck create confusion, depression, fear, panic and loss of touch with what is real.

The fastest way for me to become depressed and fearful is to think depressing and fearful thoughts. If I spend time thinking on a past painful hurt, soon feelings of anger, bitterness and revenge come back to life. Thinking about what scares me feeds my nervousness, worry and even panic. But, a favorite place or memory of mine can elicit calmness and relaxation. Meditation on God's love and faithfulness brings peace and tranquility. As a statement on the wall of a YMCA reminded me, "Mental well-being is a condition to be achieved and maintained."

I must learn to choose my thoughts like I choose the clothes I wear. I don't go to my closet and grab any blouse or pants. I choose carefully to look my best each day. My thoughts need to be selected with vigilance also, for they will determine the appearance of my personality and character.

After my mind becomes set on a thought, I soon act on it. I have analyzed and rationalized and am ready to experience it. My thoughts and associated experiences form my personality and character by becoming my habits. What my mind thinks on the most becomes strong and what I fail to entertain and make important becomes weak. If I rarely think positively, pessimism and negativity govern my reasoning. Optimism and hopefulness appear foolish. What I hear and see, who and what I spend time with, tips the ever-sensitive balance of what is true and what is bogus. When error reigns supreme and clamps its iron jaws around my mind, I begin to believe things that are not based on reason or fact.

When I deny and refuse to work on my problems, my mind has to do strange things in an effort to keep me functioning. Part of me fights to hold on to the lies and untruths. My other part struggles to give me the courage to listen and consider the unfamiliar. Whatever part I choose to let influence me becomes the stronger part, growing larger and controlling more areas of my life.

My thoughts can gain even more power when I verbalize them. The words I speak either build up or tear down the foundations of truth I am trying to build for myself. My words can yank the chains tighter that keep me in bondage or can begin freeing me to move toward wholeness. I declare with my mouth who I am and therefore who I believe I can become.

My belief about my disease determined my outcome. If I maintain there is no hope, then there is none for me. If I choose to believe things can get better and will, then I see that exhibited in my life. Jesus made a powerful statement when He gave two blind men the explanation for their healing. Jesus asked the blind men if they really believed He could heal them. And they said, "Why, yes, Master!" He then touched their eyes and said, *"Become what you believe."* Matthew 9:28-29, The Message. (Italics are added.) As a child of sixteen and again when my marriage failed, I believed I was unlovable, no good and deserved the worst punishment imaginable. I became that person. Some twenty years later, I now believe I am useful, loved by God and man, and am a new person. My reliance on God's power changed me just as remarkably as the blind men were able to see.

My ability to heal also depended on my willingness to put into words what was going on inside of me. What uncharted territory this was for me! Seemed as scary as the jungles of Africa at night would be. Sounded as uncomfortable for me as flying in a fighter jet over enemy territory. So scary and uncomfortable for me as a child that I never learned to do it until in my thirties. Sometimes I swore I would never do it again when I was misunderstood or treated harshly. This was one of the keys that unlocked my chains.

What was inside of me had to come out so I could look at it and study it for accuracy and reality. My beliefs had to be examined and confronted in love. When I kept things to myself, problems grew and festered. Lies became truth. My unchallenged perceptions became reality. Anger graduated to hate, and hate majored in revenge.

Talking can be like opening the infected, gangrenous wound to let the poison out. A caring and honest friend can be the salve that soothes and helps speed the healing process. Who I really was and wanted to be was in there somewhere yearning to get out and striving to be free from all that hindered me.

I began talking and sharing my deepest thoughts much like learning to be comfortable around water. First, I tested the temperature of water with my toe. I was tentative. If the temperature was just right and the depth and sparkle just the way I liked it, I took someone's hand and ventured in with them. One day I put both feet in. The next time up to my knees. I had to play a long time in the shallow end with my friend before I'd venture any deeper. The day I went to the deep end with my friend and did not worry about my toes having to touch the bottom was the day I began to taste the freedom to be the person I truly was. Now I can speak openly and honestly and trust that it's good and OK to be who I am. Being happy with who I am and having fun being that person is what playing in the deep end is all about. Taking risks and welcoming challenges is like diving off the high dive or going to the bottom to retrieve the quarter first. There are always new dives to try and new water games for me to play if I am willing. This word picture helps me visualize the progress made in my life.

It took a big risk to finally share. It was a step of faith. But in the sharing of the personal without holding anything back, came a great healing. It was with one friend in particular, although several loved me constant through the years. She listened to everything that I had to say. She listened to the same things again and again and always had time for me. She didn't judge me or try to change me, but accepted me wholeheartedly just the way I was. Even after I told her the very worst and weird that I could tell her, she remained the same. Nothing changed except me. Because she first loved me without criticalness, I could accept it later when she spoke of better ways to do things. She loved me like my mother and father were unable to do for me. She loved me without any conditions attached and that enabled me to begin loving myself. I learned that I was indeed loveable and I deserved better than I had believed. Now I am freed to be the person I am and not the person I thought I had to be in order to be loved. I don't have to be perfect and I don't have to measure up to someone else's expectations. And I can handle it when someone doesn't like me or doesn't agree with what I say. It's OK to be different. It's good to be the unique person God intended me to be.

Affirmations From God's Word

We lead every thought and purpose away captive into the obedience of Christ, the Messiah, the Anointed One. *II Corinthians 10:5*

Search me (thoroughly), O God, and know my heart! Try me and know my thoughts! And see if there is any wicked or hurtful way in me, and lead me in the way everlasting. *Psalm 139: 23, 24*

Set your minds and hearts on all the words which I command you this day, that you may command them to your children, that they may be watchful to do all the words of the law. For it is not an empty and worthless trifle for you; it is your very life. *Deuteronomy 32:46, 47*

And God's peace which transcends all understanding shall garrison and mount guard over your hearts and minds in Christ Jesus. Whatever is true, whatever is worthy of reverence and is honorable and seemly, whatever is just, whatever is pure, whatever is lovely and lovable, whatever is kind and winsome and gracious, if there is any virtue and excellence, if there is anything worthy of praise, think on and weigh and take account of these things (fix your minds on them). *Philippians 4:7, 8.*

For as he thinks in his heart, so is he. *Proverbs 23:7*

A gentle tongue with it's healing power is a tree of life. *Proverbs 15:4*

Death and life are in the power of the tongue, and they who indulge in it shall eat the fruit of it for death or life. *Proverbs 18:21*

And you will know the Truth, and the Truth will set you free. *John 8:32*

Reflective Reassurance

In a matter of a couple minutes, one thought can put me in touch with one hundred thoughts that are increasingly more detailed and off base. Habitually setting my heart on things of excellence and virtue enables me to influence the state of my mind. That is why God's ways shape my very life and who I am. When I change what I think on, I can change me.

Chapter 4
I Don't Need A Therapist!
Our necessity: the conduit to God

The responsibility as an adult for my well-being lies with myself. Not an institution. Not a hospital. Not the government. Not a therapist or a psychiatrist. Not even friends and family. Certainly each of these are helpful and needed at times. But the ultimate and foremost responsibility for change and health lie with me. I am my own responsibility.

William Glasser in *Reality Therapy* asserts that people do not act irresponsibly because they are ill; but rather, they stay ill because they have learned to act irresponsibly. He believes that teaching a person he is sick is teaching him to be a passive participant in whatever treatment the physician recommends.

I learned that I was not a passive participant at the mercy of doctors and the many side effects of medications. I am responsible for who I have become and who I can become. It is my responsibility to actively make choices that promote my healing. It is up to me whether I stay where I am or if I progress and overcome. The more responsible my choices, the more responsible my behavior becomes. My choices are based on my beliefs, that are in turn the products of my self-talk and my perception of the world around me. When these become lined up with the truth of God's Word, my behavior will begin to edify myself and those around me.

Being responsible for my own well being was an overwhelming thought as a seriously ill person. How could I ever be expected to heal my own sick mind? How was I ever going to be up to such an overwhelming task when I was the one in the middle of it? I couldn't be my own therapist and doctor. Could there actually be a way out of this tangled mess? Yes, there was a way. But paradoxically, it was just the opposite of all the ways I thought would work. Instead of trying to be the one with all the answers, I had to give up trying. Herein I found hope and answers. For when I admitted I was helpless and incapable of doing such an impossible work, I was ready to begin.

My healing began with looking outside myself for spiritual help. I did not have a need for a power greater than myself until I first knew I didn't have the answers and I was incapable of solving my problems. I required Someone much bigger and much better than myself.

I discovered that power greater than myself is God. He planned and knit me carefully and patiently together in my mother's womb. He lovingly considered each stitch that would create a unique life of beauty and usefulness. God knew what it would take to quiet my fears. He was not confused by outward appearances; but knew my history in detail, clearly seeing the origins of my hurt. Because He comprehended my weaknesses and strengths, His help was individually tailored to my specific needs. He knew what issue to work on first and exactly how and when to approach it.

God does not rely on the latest fads in therapy for He is Wisdom. He is the Perfect Counselor, not treating me according to standard procedure, or needing to consult others or wonder which diagnostic tools might be appropriate. He has all the answers for He is the Answer. He is not concerned about keeping the client-therapist relationship within business hours or within definite boundaries. He is available anytime, anywhere and for any reason, dealing with me in a personal relationship that exudes love. He has collected all my tears and saved them in a bottle. I am always on His mind, and in the palm of each hand, He has tattooed a picture of me.

And what did He ask of me? Only to come to Him and give Him what weighed me down so heavily and kept me from being all that I was created to become. Come to Him as a child comes to a loving father. Climb up on His lap. I laid my head against His chest and let His arms hold me close. Feel His strength, His love and His caring. I wasn't afraid to tell Him everything. I started from the beginning and told him all about my life. I looked in His face and saw His tears for me. Good fathers are trustworthy and never betray their children. I let Him love me, comfort me and give me what I needed. My Heavenly Father wanted what was best for me and promised to give me the desires of my heart. And what does He ask in return for all of this? Just my love.

How did I ever learn to give love to a God I could not see and did not trust? I learned by first letting God give me love. His love for me made the messed up parts of my life move back into their correct places. I learned to love unconditionally, forgive, and desire the good of others above myself by letting God love, forgive and bless me with His best. God yearns to do for us, and give us answers to our problems.

Learning to trust God takes time and patience and requires building a loving friendship. We learn of God through reading His Word. We learn to trust Him as a friend when we begin to apply His Word to our daily life. We gain greater understanding as we read what other Christians have written about His ways. Through prayer we find that God does listen and care about us. We learn He does do exactly what He says He will do and that He is trustworthy. Knowing and trusting a friend deepens and becomes sweeter as the years go by. As I shared more and more experiences with my friends, I found them to be true to their word. It was no different getting to know God and having Him become my best Friend - the One I talked to first.

God used others to show me what He is like. He enticed me by giving a part of Himself through someone I knew. Finding faithfulness, forgiveness, and unconditional love in a friend taught me what I could expect from God. There was no gift greater than friends who loved me no matter what -- who did not seek to criticize or change me, but invited me to be glad to be myself.

One of God's most healing gifts were friends that I could say anything to and knew that they listened carefully. A cathartic, healthy talk caused positive changes in my mind, body and spirit. Nothing communicated caring as much as listening. By listening, my friends said that I was valuable, and what I had to say was significant. In the words of George Eliot, "Oh, the comfort, the inexpressible comfort of feeling safe with a person: having neither to weigh thoughts nor measure words, but to pour them out."

During my first visit to a therapist as an adult in my early thirties, I was totally amazed when she began writing down what I said to her and asking questions. I could not believe that someone thought my words were worth remembering and clarifying. How I viewed myself was directly related to having friends and therapists listen to me unconditionally.

When I knew that someone truly loved me and that love would not change because of what I did or said, I could begin to trust sharing my hurts, fears, and dreams. Pretending or hiding wasn't necessary anymore because I was loved for who I was. I could admit mistakes and still feel secure. Laughing at myself became easier because I was held in high regard without needing to change or pretend. When I understood that being human and fallible was good, then messing up was no longer a big deal. I was no longer on a roller coaster ride of feelings that could make me or break me depending on what people said about me or what I thought they said. Rather, I began to believe in myself and to have confidence in who I was. Protecting myself from possible hurt and rejection was no longer an automatic response because I did not gain love by pleasing others.

My friends could be trusted to deal with me honestly and for my best interest. Their desire was to help and incite me to mature in wisdom and healthiness. They continually pointed me back to God, knowing that He alone had the power and wisdom to change me into something beautiful and worthy of praise. This was what healed my distrust of others. It enabled me to let go of self-hatred.

I first had to see and experience God in other people before I was ready to actually deal with God one on one. My love and trust was betrayed by humans and had to be restored by humans before I could love an unseen and sometimes hard-to-understand God.

An extensive study showed the presence of common elements in recoverers from mental disorders such as schizophrenia. A lot of recoverers have a mentor, someone they trust and who cares. They also have someone who believes in them and says they have a chance to get better and they have found a safe, decent place to live, rather than being out on the streets (*Monitor on Psychology*, Feb. 2000). There is tremendous healing power in the act of genuine friendship and love.

Even a loving relationship with God and friends does not silence the doubting and wondering completely. How good could ever come from the confusion and sorrow I knew so well remained a mystery until one evening. I cried to God again about the disease that had brought so much grief. I said, "Oh, God, this weakness is so ugly to me. I've tried so long and hard to change it and make it go away. To the world, it seems so bad that it scares people away. It is unacceptable and not talked about. Even I only talk about it with those I trust most fully, and then sometimes I wonder if they chuckle behind my back."

God answered most quietly, "My dear child, I made you the way you are. I formed you and put you together this very way."

"But, why God?" I cried out to Him.

"So I could use you."

"But, how can you use me the way I am, so weak and broken and many times confused?"

"Many ways my child. Just be still and you will see."

That evening brought a quiet peace across my mind and my life that left a confident knowing in my heart that all was well. I do my best to trust and rest in Him; but there are times I doubt and cause myself more grief. Each time God lovingly brings all of Himself to fresh and sweet remembrance for me.

Affirmations From God's Word

I call heaven and earth to witness this day against you that I have set before you life and death, the blessings and the curses; therefore choose life, that you and your descendants may live and may love the Lord your God, obey His voice, and cling to Him. For He is your life and the length of your days. *Deuteronomy 30:19,20*

Oil and perfume rejoice the heart; so does the sweetness of a friend's counsel that comes from the heart. *Proverbs 27:9*

A friend loves at all times, and is born, as a brother, for adversity. *Proverbs 17:17*

For the Lord God is a Sun and Shield; the Lord bestows present grace and favor and future glory, honor, splendor, and heavenly bliss! No good thing will He withhold from those who walk uprightly. *Psalms 84:11*

Trust, lean on, rely on, and be confident in the Lord and do good; so shall you dwell in the land and feed surely on His faithfulness, and truly you shall be fed. Delight yourself also in the Lord and He will give you the desires and secret petitions of your heart. Commit your way to the Lord, roll and repose each care of your load on Him; trust, lean on, rely on, and be confident also in Him and He will bring it to pass. And He will make your uprightness and right standing with God go forth as the light, and your justice and right as the shining sun of the noonday. Be still and rest in the Lord; wait for Him and patiently lean yourself upon Him. *Psalm 37:3-7*

For I know well the plans I have in mind for you, says the Lord, plans for your welfare, not for disaster! Plans to give you a future full of hope. When you call me, when you go to pray to me, I will listen to you. When you look for me, you will find me. Yes, when you seek me with all your heart, you will find me with you, says the

Lord. *Jeremiah 29:11-14*

Come close to God and He will come close to you. *James 4:8*

For You did form my inward parts; You did knit me together in my mother's womb. I will confess and praise You for You are fearful and wonderful and for the awful wonder of my birth! Wonderful are Your works, and that my inner self knows right well. My frame was not hidden from You when I was being formed in secret and intricately and curiously wrought as if embroidered with various colors in the depths of the earth which is a region of darkness and mystery. Your eyes saw my unformed substance, and in Your book all the days of my life were written before ever they took shape, when as yet there was none of them. How precious and weighty also are Your thoughts to me, O God! How vast is the sum of them. If I could count them, they would be more in number than the sand. *Psalms 138:13-18*

Exercise foresight and be on the watch to look (after one another), to see that no one falls back and fails to secure God's grace (His unmerited favor and spiritual blessing), in order that no root of resentment (rancor, bitterness, or hatred) shoots forth and causes trouble and bitter torment; *Hebrews 12:15*

In my distress I cried to the Lord, and He answered me. *Psalm 120:1*

Before I formed you in the womb I knew and approved of you as My chosen instrument, and before you were born I separated and set you apart, consecrating you. *Jeremiah 1:5*

(And the Lord answered) Can a woman forget her nursing child, that she should not have compassion on the son of her womb? Yes, they may forget, yet I will not forget you. Behold, I have indelibly imprinted (tattooed a picture of) you on the palm of each of My hands. *Isaiah 49:15,16*

You have seen me tossing and turning through the night. You have collected all my tears and preserved them in your bottle! You have recorded every one in your book. This one thing I know: God is for me! *Psalms 56:8,9*

Reflective Reassurance

If we could only understand how much God loves us. If only we could believe that He means no harm. That He waits with outstretched arms eager to give us the desires of our heart. Help us Lord to understand and believe.

Chapter 5
I Can't Help It! This Is the Way I Was Made.
To change or stay the same is the decision of a lifetime.

When my mind was hanging on to anger, bitterness and unforgiveness, my body was hanging onto it also. Every cell responds to the intense grip of emotions that destroy. Negative feelings eat away at the physical body, the mental processes and the spiritual capabilities. The erosion did not limit itself to me; but it reached out to harm whatever and whomever it touched. According to Christiane Northrup, M.D. in *Women's Bodies, Women's Wisdom,* "But now we know that our body organs communicate directly with the brain and vice versa, through chemical messengers known as neuropeptides...What this means is that our entire body feels and expresses emotion - all parts of us 'think' and 'feel.'"

My hurts stayed buried deeply under the rubble of years of pretending, hiding and protecting myself. I may have spent a lifetime acting like all was well. For the most part, I was still a child -- in a grown up body. Hiding in my career, shopping, children, spouse's life, or in a myriad of other havens became a way of life. Defending myself from everything that appeared remotely similar to the people and the situations that hurt me was a quick and automatic response. The behaviors I used to keep myself safe became strange and unpredictable. Such elaborate defense strategies were devised that I became unbalanced and unable to function in my daily life.

These unique ways of coping concealed my real issues. Symptoms developed that seemed totally unrelated to my past and present. An example would be the need to feel in complete control of situations. But to one who understands, my fears, anxiety and lack of trust of others were the reasons for needing to be in control. I was mistakenly convinced that I was not an angry person and that I had no reason to be depressed. Rigid, black and white thinking revealed pride, stubbornness and lack of compassion. My attitudes and expectations gave my secrets away. Past and present relationships with others shouted out my own painful history. It didn't matter what I did, where I went, and who I was with -- I eventually hit again and again the brick wall of my unresolved past. For I learned when I buried emotions, I buried them alive. They were like smoking embers. Therefore, leaving negative emotions unexpressed is dangerous, not simply having them.

When my brother married, I flew to St. Louis alone to attend his wedding. As I went through the receiving line, I greeted his new wife with a hug and a congratulatory welcome into our family. Then I stepped toward my brother to greet him. No sooner did our eyes meet, than I began to cry out hysterically and run. As soon as I got out of the building, I calmed down immediately and I had no idea where the panic had come from or why. Expressing emotion was out of character for me and it appeared unrelated to anything going on in my life.

Two friends and I were visiting. I began putting lipstick on in a way they thought funny. Rather than moving the lipstick across my lips, I was holding the tube still and moving my head. They doubled over in laughter. I became silent and began twirling my hair. They attempted to talk to me, but I would not answer. They stopped laughing, but I remained silent. Fear crossed time and space from years before when I was rejected in favor of a new brother. When we bury our feelings, worries and hurts, they will rise again. When they do, they appear to have nothing to do with today's problems and circumstances.

The course of my disease was determined by the degree to which I was willing to fight to grow and overcome. The desire to change had to be a burning desire that nothing could stop. There were times that I did not prosper in health and wisdom because I refused to risk examining my thoughts and actions for error. The hatred of my Mom and Dad lasted from the age of ten until my late forties. I felt justified in my anger. I rejected changing what sought to kill me. I preferred to stay where I was with the familiar rather than have the courage to face and fight my demons.

Sometimes it seemed easier to just leave things alone and hope they would go away. This response became far too common as my son failed in school and physically acted out his own anger. I had to act for the ultimate good of all concerned, not for the immediate moment. It required love to lay aside my fears and my self-will and testify in court that my son was out of control. It took courage to look him in the eye and name the acts of rebellion for the judge that had occurred while he was in my home. Later, I changed the locks on my house and went to live with a friend for a month so that my son would be forced to make his own way.

I started changing in little ways and then continued to build on my accomplishments. It seemed I took two steps forward and then one back as I strained to develop toward spiritual and emotional maturity. Change is usually a process. It is also not something we can do in our own strength. The battle was not mine. It belonged to God. God's power and His Word transformed me into a new creature, comparable to being born again as a totally new person.

Encouragement, support and confrontation was invaluable as I struggled to learn new ways of dealing with my problems. Loving, caring and committed friends are God's most wonderful gift at any time; but especially when we are exploring new ideas and behaviors.

My friends challenged me to look at past events and people from new perspectives. My view was warped by the destructive forces of anger and revenge. Anger constructed my thoughts and gave motivation for my words and actions. I began learning about compassion and assuming the best and not the worst. Rather than insisting people misused me, I understood my thinking was wrong and that it could be changed.

In *Help Yourself to Happiness*, Dr. Maxie C. Maultsby, Jr. says,

"...people have three choices about their anger: 1. when to get angry; 2. how much to get angry; 3. how long to stay angry. They also have those same choices about any other emotion." He also states, "...an emotion is merely an inner urge to act; you don't have to act on it." He goes on to say, " Since you control your thoughts, you alone control your emotional feelings. How rationally you control them is your personal choice."

How exciting! How wonderful to know I had the power to do something about my anger and other emotions! I could decide to be in control of them rather than have them control me! And with God's help and direction, my efforts could be life-giving rather than life-destroying.

This is not to say it was easy to change; but I was definitely willing. I began by not blaming my feelings, or what I did about my problems on anyone else. I learned only my beliefs about a situation could trigger my emotions. I began to take responsibility for where I was each day. Would I become better? Or would I choose to stay where I was? It was entirely up to me.

Affirmations From God's Word

For we are not wrestling with flesh and blood (contending only with physical opponents), but against the despotisms, against the powers, against the master spirits who are the world leaders of this present darkness, against the spirit forces of wickedness in the heavenly (supernatural) sphere. *Ephesians 6:12*

All has been heard: the end of the matter is: Fear God (revere and worship Him, knowing that He is) and keep His commandments, for this is the whole of man, (the full, original purpose of His creation, the object of God's providence, the root of character, the foundation of all happiness, the adjustment to all inharmonious circumstances and conditions under the sun) and the whole (duty) for every man. *Ecclesiastics 12:13*

All the congregation of the Israelites moved on from the Wilderness of Sin by stages. *Exodus 17:1*

Reflective Reassurance

The reason to work out our problems encompasses more than our desire for contentment and success here on earth. A spiritual war rages and the victor's spoils will not be a nest egg in the bank and some nice heirloom furnishings to keep in the family. The bounty will be eternal rewards – so amazing that no one's ever seen, heard or imagined anything like it before. (I Corinthians 2:9)

Make sure that you progress daily toward the prize of eternal life. Do not let anything or anyone impede your safe passage. At times the steps toward our promised land seem small and insignificant; but every journey, no matter how long and hard, is completed one step and one problem at a time.

Chapter 6
Me Forgive? Never!
Forgiveness is a must for emotional health.

According to Thomas Jefferson, "Honesty is the first chapter of the book of wisdom." And William Glasser, MD. tells us, "The only means by which...(a person) ...can become motivated to change is to look honestly at his own behavior to determine whether or not it contributes to fulfilling his needs."

God's Word tells us, "I acknowledged my sin to You, and my iniquity I did not hide. I said, I will confess my transgressions to the Lord (continually unfolding the past till all is told) -- then You (instantly) forgave me the guilt and iniquity of my sin. Selah (pause, and calmly think of that)!" Psalm 32:5 "If we freely admit that we have sinned and confess our sins, He is faithful and just (true to His own nature and promises) and will forgive our sins (dismiss our lawlessness) and (continually) cleanse us from all unrighteousness (everything not in conformity to His will in purpose, thought, and action)." I John 1:9.

I learned that healing could begin only with transparent honesty. And I learned honesty by challenging everything with what God was saying to me in the Bible and through family and friends. I listened and considered deeply what loved ones told me about myself. They could see more clearly than I did.

When I hid nothing and was painfully honest, I had made a good beginning. Without honesty, I would have stayed stuck where I was. I had to stop denying I had problems or sin. "If we say we have no sin (refusing to admit we are sinners), we delude and lead ourselves astray, and the Truth (which the Gospel presents) is not in us (does not dwell in our hearts). I John 1:8.

Blaming others for my problems was a choice to stay stuck and full of self-pity. I no longer saw my parents or situations concerning them clearly. The lack of honest appraisal meant I had no shame or remorse about the hatred of my Mom and Dad. I slowly started the process of physical and spiritual decay. My life began to fall apart as my mind became ridden with disease. Honesty was the only antidote for deception.

Forgiveness has been a hard lesson for me to learn and remember. Some things have been easy for me to forgive and others seem almost impossible. I made categories in my mind for the different sins. There was a list of easy to forgive sins and the big, unforgivable ones. Learning to forgive myself and others have been major obstacles to finding rest for my mind.

It is not uncommon for emotional problems to be rooted in unforgiveness. According to Steve Fine, a minister and counselor, "The two main issues I see in counseling people with emotional problems are forgiving themselves and forgiving others."

It was here that my line to God's peace through forgiveness got tangled and snapped in the debris of self-centered guilt and blame. I was sure that my sins were so great that I did not deserve to live. The failure of my marriage, the reoccurrence of the schizophrenia, what I had done as a result to my children -- were unforgivable sins. I believed I caused the problems and took full responsibility, plus some, for everything. If I had only said this or done that differently, I could have changed attitudes and saved the marriage. If I had only been stronger, the schizophrenia would not have reoccurred. In other words, if I had done everything right, there would not have been any problems in our little family. It was all me, no one else was to blame. I deserved what had happened; and it didn't get better because I didn't do enough and I didn't do anything good enough.

Not only did I feel fully responsible; but also fully capable of fixing and changing others and circumstances, if they would just listen. God wasn't necessary, for in my mind I had the ability to make everything better. I believed I could and should have done the very things only God can do. I had an elevated view of myself and my abilities. I thought I knew what other people needed and how the present and future should be. Since then, God has shown me so many times that He has things under control and not me. Most of the time, I do not have a clue to what another person needs. I only get in God's way if I think I do.

The guilt and shame in my life was so great that I had to fix people to make up for all the wrong I had done. My son lied, stole and was abusive. If I could fix my son, people would see how good I really was, and I would be able to prove my worth. I needed to fix for my sake, not for the sake of others. I had to prove my excellence to atone for my mistakes.

When my son's father was involved in his life and doing things for his benefit, I became jealous and possessive of my son. It was my job to help him and only I should do the saving. Proving that I really was not the bad mother was so important that it controlled what I did and thought.

God needed to change me before I could be of use to anyone. He left me in painful situations until I was willing to be shaped and molded to His liking. He loved me enough to let me hurt until I turned back to Him. I am so glad He did.

As we look at ourselves honestly, we must also learn the truth about God's forgiveness -- refreshing ourselves again and again in the cooling balm of His Word. We must teach our children God's truth at every stage and situation in their life. God's truths heal and set free. Ignorance of God's words bring sickness, worry, despair, depression and eventual death.

When we do not understand the foundational truth of God's forgiveness and determine to believe it, we run the risk of losing our minds. When we say God's forgiveness does not cover certain things, we open the door wide to fears and confusion. For me, being out of touch with reality sometimes began in this way.

Sin, in thought, word or deed, separates us from God. To a holy

God, there are no differences in sins. There are no degrees or categories. The only way we could ever please God is to be holy and sinless like Himself.

But, this same God says He will forgive any sin. There is no sin too great to forgive because Jesus satisfied God's demands on man to be holy and spotless. Because of Jesus, God can look on us. And when He looks on us, He sees Christ's holiness draped over and covering our stain-filled life. All is forgiven not because of who we are, what we do, how good we are, or how we have tried to make up for our sins; but because Jesus fulfilled God's requirements of death as the penalty for sin.

If we refuse to forgive ourselves, it is because we have chosen unforgiveness instead of God's plan which makes all things right between God and us. The forgiveness is there waiting for us to reach out and take. We can choose not to accept it. That is the only sin that is not forgivable because God has provided everything, and we refuse to believe and accept the truth of His gift. If we say our sins are somehow different or too great, we set ourselves up as God and say we know better that He. There is no truth in that and no freedom from the curses of sin on our life here and in eternity.

No loophole exists to make a certain sin not covered by the cross. We cannot shock or derail God by what we have done, said or thought. God does not give us second or third best because of our sins. He offers compassion when we confess. He convicts so that He can show us His mercy. All of His wrath and anger was settled at the cross. He has let go of His anger. We are the ones who hold on to it and keep punishing ourselves. God made peace with us a long time ago. It's time now to make peace with Him and with ourselves.

Forgiving can be compared to peeling an onion, in that it is done layer by layer. Circumstances will come up and it will seem that we are back to square one. We feel like we've learned nothing from our past. But when we look more closely, we see that we have made progress. Our negative attitude doesn't last quite as long. Or perhaps we stopped before saying something hurtful that we would have quickly said in the past. Maybe our pity party is over a little bit earlier than the last one. And like peeling onions, many tears are shed when we let go of old ways and old perspectives. We are losing thoughts and behaviors that have been familiar, comfortable and predictable for us through the years. It can be like saying goodbye to old friends.

Affirmations From God's Word

(Even the migratory birds are punctual to their seasons.) Yes, the stork (excelling in the great height of her flight) in the heavens knows her appointed times (of migration), and the turtledove, the swallow, and the crane observe the time of their return. But my people do not know the law of the Lord (which the lower animals instinctively recognize in so far as it applies to them). *Jeremiah 8:7*

I would return My people from their captivity in which they are slaves to the misery brought on by their own sins. *Hosea 6:11*

Do not be conformed to this world (this age), fashioned after and adapted to its external, superficial customs, but be transformed (changed) by the (entire) renewal of your mind (by its new ideals and its new attitude) so that you may prove (for yourselves) what is the good and acceptable and perfect will of God even the thing which is good and acceptable and perfect (in His sight for you).

He who does not use his endeavors to heal himself is brother to him who commits suicide. *Proverbs 18:9*

...Do not merely desire peaceful relations with God, with your fellowmen, and with yourself, but pursue, go after them! *I Peter 3:11*

...for by whatever anyone is made inferior or worse or is overcome, to that person or thing he is enslaved. *II Peter 2:19*

The Lord will fight for you, and you shall hold your peace and remain at rest. *Exodus 14:14.*

The Lord is close to those who are of a broken heart and saves such as are crushed with sorrow for sin and are humbly and thoroughly penitent. *Psalms 34:18*

So any person who knows what is right to do but does not do it, to him it is sin. *James 4:17*

For You, O Lord, are good, and ready to forgive our trespasses, sending them away, letting them go completely and forever; and You are abundant in mercy and loving-kindness to all those who call upon You. *Psalm 86:5*

Reflective Reassurance

The first and most important step in the healing process is honesty and forgiveness. No one could do this for me. If I skipped or circumvented this act, I would have missed it all. Refusing to heal ourselves compares to committing suicide. Those are some very strong words. I had to decide what to do with them – act on them or ignore them. It's a choice many of us will be asked to make at some point in our life.

Chapter 7
Trying to be Perfect Is Mistake #1
Measuring up silences uniqueness.

My husband had been my god. He determined right and wrong for me as I did whatever I thought would please him. I lived my life according to what I believed he wanted and expected. When our two children became school age, my husband asked me if I thought they should attend public or parochial school. He prefaced his question with his opinion that he saw no great benefit going to parochial school when public school was free. Because I already knew his desire before I answered, I just agreed with him. I neglected to express my views in favor of parochial school. I really expect that my husband would have listened to my thoughts and even gone along with many of them, but I rarely gave him the opportunity. Because I would not state my beliefs or stand up for them, the marriage appeared dominated by him. Many opportunities were lost to grow and mature in our relationship because I did not take on the role of working as a team in our marriage. I was a nonperson expecting all my needs to be met in him.

As we reached the fourteenth year of our marriage, I allowed my husband to become more important than God when I chose his desires over what I knew was morally right. It was more important to keep him loving me. God made sure my world was shaken and the rug was pulled from under my feet. He loved me enough to make sure I didn't continue to want to please a man more than I did Him.

My children suffered because of the schizophrenia, depression and later our divorce. The relationship I had with my son and daughter was over in many ways. They were left to drift aimlessly without family, structure or predictability. I was almost like an absentee Mom as I spent most of my time in bed. Basically on their own, my thirteen year old daughter took charge, doing her best to hold things together. My son, who was eleven, began turning to his peers for support and understanding, which eventually led to using and selling drugs. My daughter scolded me, lectured me, and gave advice and commands on how I should handle her brother. Then she made sure I followed through. She became the parent and I the child. As I depended on her to be the adult, her anger and disgust toward me grew intense. Through gritted teeth, my daughter said she hated me and never wanted to be anything like me. She moved out in her junior year of high school. The reversed roles and anger continued well into her adulthood.

Everything I dreamed of for myself and my family had slipped through my fingers and was gone. And it was my fault. My plans in life had been to be the perfect mother and wife. My family would have no problems and would be blessed because of me. The standard punishment—death—was not enough for me. The voices told me again that I was so bad, so despicable; that I would become what was hated the worst above everything – the Antichrist. The person who would deceive and turn the world against God, and torture and destroy God's people, became me.

Perfectionism

A very large part of me believed I was perfect. I had to believe it. Nothing else was acceptable. If I wasn't perfect, I was a complete failure, utterly worthless and the scum of the earth. I just had to do better and try harder to be good enough. I never gave up. That was a sign of weakness. I never admitted mistakes. I dared not. They were not allowed. I attributed to God the same standards and perspectives that I used to judge myself.

During one Christmas season, friends of my parents came to visit. They went to the front door that was rarely used. Only salesmen or other strangers would knock on this door. Because the living room was small, the Christmas tree was placed in the corner against the door. My Mom opened the door slightly to tell the friends to use the breezeway door that came into the kitchen. In doing so, the tree fell to the floor and ornaments were scattered all around. It was only a short distance to the other door, maybe twenty steps. It seemed we all jumped up knowing what to do without needing a word from our parents. We scurried quickly and quietly to fix this mishap. My Dad went to the other door to greet our guests. When the friends came inside, the tree was in order and we were all seated in our places as if nothing had ever happened. The topic of discussion was the weather. The fallen tree was never mentioned to the friends. This pictures clearly how our family worked together to make things appear just right to outsiders. Mistakes could not be talked about or approached with humor. They were serious and had to be hidden.

I was caught in the extremes. There was no middle ground. Everything was black and white, perfect or completely evil and defiled. Anthony Storr, the author of *Human Aggression,* states: "The majority of paranoid schizophrenics are unable to express their hostility except in fantasy. There is some attempt to maintain self-esteem by grandiose fantasy. To be the subject of widespread attention, even if it be malicious, implies that one is an important person. They feel powerless to resist the evil intention of others, especially since their persecutors are often imagined to possess special powers. At the same time, they believe themselves to be very important. Grandiose ideas serve to preserve or salvage tottering self-esteem."

I was admitted to Baptist Hospital during Christmas break in 1981. I walked the halls proclaiming that I was Jesus. After I went in another patient's room declaring who I was and what I could do, staff intervened and occupied me elsewhere. One day my son's ear was hurting, and I took him to the bathroom to "heal" him. I quoted a biblical phrase, put my fingers in his ears, and as Jesus, declared him healed.

Signs beside the road riveted my attention. It was hard to pull my eyes away to watch the road and drive. I had assigned each letter a value, similar to Scrabble letters. I had to add each word up to find the total value. The word was good if the value for it was in multiples of five. Multiples of ten were acceptable, but fives were the best. Then the value of all the words together had to be added up to see if the phrase or sentence was good. Even when I tried to stop, this was something I had to do.

My concentration was poor. Watching a movie or anything on TV was too hard. My thoughts and preoccupations were much stronger. I frequently ran out of gas while driving, as I spent more time thinking than paying attention to the real world.

Numbers scared me. The three sixes in my account number with the utility company put me in a panic every month. I knew the reason that number had been assigned to me. It was a sign of things to come.

I chose to do things that could be rehearsed and practiced beforehand. Nothing was done spontaneously. Life was serious; and everybody, it seemed, was watching and grading me.

Even if I felt I could do something well, I memorized it. But because I couldn't trust myself to say it right or remember it, I read every word verbatim. It had to be right or it was absolutely no good. I always preferred the written word because I could change it until I got it just right. There was time to hunt down the perfect word and a message could be delivered when I chose to send it.

There were only certain things I could talk about without shutting down emotionally and physically. At each session with one therapist I brought a list of items to talk about. This was the way I felt safe and in control. She allowed me to do this and did not bring up anything different although no other client had ever brought a list.

I didn't enjoy or welcome unplanned phone calls. There wasn't time to think about what I wanted to say or how I wanted to say it. I needed to consider the caller's responses and my answers to possible questions. So I had very little to say that was meaningful and virtually nothing that was personal.

Talking about the weather and certain things about my car was safe. Other talk about my car could indicate I was not taking care of the car or driving it perfectly. It was necessary to weigh and measure everything I said. My words had to prove I was doing everything right and that my motives were pure.

If someone's comment indicated that I was doing something unacceptable or not the best way, then I focused on never doing it again, especially in their presence. I did not forget because the infraction consumed me. Everything was about me and revolved around me.

There were more reasons to be perfect after the divorce. I had to cover up tracks and prove to the world there was no sin in me. I could not come to terms with what I had done. My coping skills were no match for the huge stressors of guilt and shame. I would have to show the world that I was too good to have ever done something like that and too good to have been the reason for the marriage not working. Punishment and atonement dictated my actions for years to come.

Self-disgust did not allow me to have nice things or do good things for myself. Going without, or relying solely on garage sales and hand-me-downs, was my usual way of acquiring things. I didn't take pride in my home or care about decorating. A wall of black numbness did not allow happiness or self-indulgence. People used me and were disrespectful because I allowed it. It was what I deserved. There was no reason to stand up for myself. I simply wasn't worth it.

My Dad's words hurt much more than they ever helped. He did not believe in me. He assumed that somehow I deserved whatever happened to me. During the divorce, he wanted to know what I had done to cause it. Later, when I lost my job in public school, he assumed the innocence of the administrators rather than mine.

Reading the temperature on an indoor/outdoor thermometer seems like a little thing. But for me, it reminded me that I was not trusted or believed capable. Whenever I read the temperature, one of my parents would double-check me. Not because I couldn't read thermometers, but just because.

As children, we hear things and understand them as a child. The lack of understanding and many times the error of our understanding are never explored or questioned. We walk into adulthood with the foundation for our life misformed, unbalanced and resting on half-truths and sometimes even lies. We make decisions and face life's toughest struggles with misinformation or sometimes no information.

What a skewed and distorted view of God we sometimes have! Our recognition of who He is and what He is like can be a direct reflection of our view of ourselves and the world as we have experienced it.

There were few opportunities for truth to reach me. I could not attend church because the Antichrist or the end times might be mentioned. When going into an inspirational bookstore, I could only go directly to the section I wanted. I could not browse. I could not listen to an inspirational radio or TV program. The Antichrist fear controlled my life.

One of my errors in thinking was that God cannot be trusted. God will trick you. He will say one thing and then do another -- just because He's God and He can. He certainly proved that in my dream of becoming the Antichrist. God could do with me in the blink of an eye anything He fancied and without my foreknowledge. Against everything I thought I was. Against everything I believed in. Totally out of my control. This load-bearing wall of my foundation put an end to many dreams and any hope or peace.

I was like a ground soldier going into battle using plans and preparations intended for battle in the air. I was studying the right pages and subject, but using the wrong book.

In such a state, I was left confused, angry and not understanding why things were going wrong and why things didn't improve. I believed I was doing everything right and everything I knew to do. Why wouldn't God do His part? Why wouldn't God give me a chance? Why wouldn't life give me a break? That's all I asked for. Just a chance.

I expected God to wave His magic wand and fix everything in my life. He said He could do anything and all we had to do was ask. I didn't understand then that God's timetable is sometimes very different from ours. He is always working and preparing the way for us, even when we cannot see it being done.

Affirmations From God's Word

For He is not a God of confusion and disorder but of peace and order. *I Corinthians 14:33*

Now where there is absolute remission (forgiveness and cancellation of the penalty) of these (sins and lawbreaking), there is no longer any offering made to atone for sin. *Hebrews 10:18*

The thief comes only in order to steal and kill and destroy. I came that they may have and enjoy life, and have it in abundance and to the full, till it overflows. *John 10:10*

Fear not (there is nothing to fear) for I am with you; do not look around you in terror and be dismayed, for I am your God, I will strengthen and harden you to difficulties, yes, I will help you; yes, I will hold you up and retain you with My victorious right hand of rightness and justice. *Isaiah 41:10-13*

Who is among you who reverently fears the Lord, who obeys the voice of His Servant, yet who walks in darkness and deep trouble and has no shining splendor in his heart? Let him rely on, trust in, and be confident in the name of the Lord, and let him lean upon and be supported by his God. *Isaiah 50:10*

Reflective Reassurance

When my thoughts become confused and I feel overwhelmed with doubts, I can be sure God is not part of them. This is the foundation for knowing what is real. It brings me back and stops the runaway ideas. If my peace is gone, I know God is also absent. When God inhabits my mind, there is no room for disorder or fear.

My mind had become a free for all with no limits or discipline—like a child out of control and gone astray. It seemed the thought that shouted the loudest got my attention. I needed to set rules and be consistent. I had to have structure and order. What thoughts would I allow in my mind? With what would I feed my mind? Which thoughts would I entertain and spend time with? Which ones would I run off and never allow back?

I stood on the precept that God loves me and everything He says is for my good. He is Truth and Wisdom. Therefore, I used His rulebook as my guide. Any thoughts in line with God's Word were my friends and ones contrary to God were my enemies. I asked God for wisdom, which He gives freely to all who ask.

My mind gets off track when I think on things not in line with God's truth and His ways. Whatever I allow in my mind is what I will experience in my mood and behavior.

Chapter 8
Pay Attention to Me! I'm Sick!
Sickness has many rewards.

As a child, I got noticed by being sick. My needs were met by being mentally ill. Schizophrenia made me special, and gave people a reason to take an interest in me. I talked about my problems for years. My life was about struggling. I had no other identity. Receiving help from others was my assurance that I was cared about and important. Staying in bed until someone coaxed me out provided evidence of their love. I just wanted someone to hold and love me like a child. I needed verification of where I stood with people continually for fear that I was losing my special place in their lives. I felt alone, different and hard to understand. Would anyone ever find worth and value in me apart from schizophrenia and my other problems?

When I was 33 years old, I was in a day treatment program for the mentally ill. I purposely decided to sit in the dark on the bathroom floor all day. When someone knocked on the door, I would come out as if finished in the bathroom. Then I would wait for the bathroom to be empty and I would continue my vigil in the darkness. That afternoon while still at the center, I started looking for a razorblade or anything sharp to hurt myself. Staff ended up transporting me to the hospital.

First, they went by my house to get all I needed. There were no clean clothes. While at the hospital for a week, I did not change clothes, shower or sponge bathe. I was too shy and withdrawn to venture out enough to ask about washing my clothes, though I knew there was a washer and dryer on our unit. It was also too intimidating to be without my clothes for that short time.

God brings situations up in our lives again and again until we choose to work through them. To my best recollection, God has brought a particular problem up seven times over the years. With certain people that I have grown close to, I have become possessive. It was essential that I maintain the most special spot in their life and that no one come in and take it away. To protect this illusion of specialness, I monitored their behavior with other people closely. For them to give others attention and hugs was a threat to me. If they whispered to someone, or touched them on the hand I became uncomfortable and anxious. I had to be privy to their conversations, lest someone else be replacing me in my friend's life. Interrupting hugs and talks were my way of protecting my perceived place in the friendship.

Even when others were hurting, I did not want my friend to show concern or affection. I also desired to know the details of my friend's life. When I knew her whereabouts and no one else did, that proved her favoritism toward me. Losing her love, or being rejected by her on any level could not be allowed; and I was always busy making sure that was not happening.

During conversations, I checked her statements to see what she was thinking of me. I measured my own words to be sure I was pleasing her and saying things the best way. If we were conversing on the phone and were interrupted, it was a sign that someone else was more important. Not having long to talk told me I was not cared about as much as someone else.

These people were all women. I transferred what I lacked and needed to them. They were placed on a pedestal and I saw them as having all the answers and being everything I needed. It was very hard to see them as doing things wrong or not being the best at everything.

As an adult wife and mother, I was intrigued by an advertised workshop on assertiveness during the lunch hour at our local library.

I listened, as the attractive woman psychologist in her thirties, shared and taught us about things that were foreign to me. I was consumed with wanting to know her and talk to her about all that was going on in my life. I was so strongly drawn to her, it was like someone else was controlling my thoughts and actions. As the meeting ended, I walked behind her, watching her every move and catching each word she said.

As she walked back to the clinic, I had the strong compulsion to ask her to ride with me so we could talk. Fearful of rejection and appearing strange, I watched her walk down the sidewalk and out of sight. Days and weeks after this workshop, she still consumed many of my waking moments. Finally, I broke down and called her. It was my first appointment with a therapist since my hospital stay as a teenager. Throughout our years of working together, I idolized her and burned with the desire for her to be pleased with me and think me the best and most special of anyone she counseled. I knew I could not be the best at getting well, so I determined to be the best at being sick and depressed.

One time she had me concentrate on a spot on the wall to relax. I sincerely became very troubled about it all. I was weak, pale and shaking. She stopped everything, giving me time to compose myself and be able to leave. When out in my car, I happened to notice her peering from behind the blinds. Although I now felt better, I put my head down on the steering wheel as if still struggling to gain control. I did this until I saw her leave. Then I drove off.

At times I knowingly worked myself up into a real down mood before I went to see her. I was assured of attention and concern that way. If I could make her worry about me and think about me while at home, I knew I was succeeding in being special and loved. I wanted her to be consumed with me as much as I was with her.

According to Anthony Storr in *Human Aggression*, it is abundantly clear that depression is accompanied by severe inhibition of the aggressive drive. "We are used to thinking of aggression as "bad" rather than regarding it as a drive which is necessary both for gaining mastery over the environment, and for separating us from each other in such a way that we do not remain over-dependent but are distinct individuals. There is an aggressive component in each of us which serves to define the territorial boundaries of each individual personality and acts against too great a mutual dependency between those who love each other." (In the paranoid schizophrenic person), "The aggressive drive towards self-assertion has been blocked at an extremely early stage in their development, with the result that almost the whole of their aggressive potential has turned to hate against a world which appears to have frustrated them from early childhood onwards."

God loves us too much not to bring up the same problem again and again in our life. We always have the choice of whether to deal with it or push it away. We will continue to encounter it until we overcome it. God gives us many opportunities to practice what we learn and to master it. All along the way, God is preparing and equipping us with all we need to rise above our problems.

As I began to change and become healthier, I had to decide if I wanted to give up this identity of sickness. I knew no other me. Would people even want to be around me if I was well? Would I be boring? Was there anything in me that people would like? I'd have to develop other reasons for people to be attracted to me and want to stay with me. Did I really want to do that? Was there anything else special about me? I vacillated back and forth, as I tried to figure out what I wanted to do and what it would cost me.

I realized we all have the need to feel important. Now I needed to decide how I was going to be important. Would my importance and sense of self continue to come from sickness? Would my role in life consist in merely being a patient? I had to choose what was going to impress me more—the disease or God's promises. I could choose to find importance in constructive and useful ways to benefit myself and others, or I could opt to stay where I was indefinitely. I decided that how I acted in the Wilderness would determine how long it would take to get to the Promised Land.

Giving up a part of me and having to replace it with something new and different was a big risk. It was difficult to know if it really would be worth the trouble and work. I had to answer some tough questions for the first time. Was life even worth living? Was there any meaning to life? Wouldn't it just be easier to call it quits and die? Life seemed much too hard most of the time. The pros and cons of each answer had to be weighed and considered. Once I determined to choose life, my struggle began to take direction and gain momentum.

I went on faith and trust at first because there was nothing else. Faith meant to believe that things would be better and problems would get smaller if I chose to change. Trust meant believing friends who told me it was worth it and that I would be glad. What if my friends were wrong? What if it was all a lie? What if it was really not worth it? I had to decide to believe what people told me and just hang on to that belief and its promises while I waited for evidence.

The psychiatrist that I saw as a sixteen-year-old said I was like a piece of very delicate china. It was so fragile that to keep it from being broken, it was kept on the top shelf where no one could reach or touch it. That is where and how it spent its life. As I thought on this and his comparison of me to the china, I decided I did not like it. I did not want to be so fragile that I could not be useful and enjoyed. I did not want others to always tiptoe around me and be careful how they handled and talked to me. I didn't know how I would do it, I just knew I wanted to be much stronger and tougher than a piece of delicate china. That little analogy became a big motivating force in my life for change.

When I was an adult in my middle thirties, my family doctor told me that I would never be able to hold down a job. He said I would have to live with someone so they could care for me. I would be incapable of living a normal life.

When I was in my late forties, another psychiatrist told me to expect my life to spiral downward as I continued to age. He explained the prognosis for schizophrenics deteriorates and declines as they become older.

Statements such as these from qualified and skilled professionals threw me into panic and despair. They caused me to question whether the progress I had made was genuine or was I only hanging on to false hopes. I had to decide whom I was going to believe -- mere men or my God. I have chosen to believe that with God the impossible is not only possible, but also obtainable.

Affirmations From God's Word

Roll your works upon the Lord (commit and trust them wholly to Him); He will cause your thoughts to become agreeable to His will, and so shall your plans be established and succeed. *Proverbs 16:3*

Fear not, for I have redeemed you (ransomed you by paying a price instead of leaving you captives); I have called you by your name; you are Mine. When you pass through the waters, I will be with you, and through the rivers, they will not overwhelm you. When you walk through the fire, you will not be burned or scorched, nor will the flame kindle upon you. For I am the Lord your God, the Holy One of Israel, your Savior. *Isaiah 43:1-3*

So be done with every trace of wickedness (depravity, malignity) and all deceit and insincerity (pretense, hypocrisy) and grudges (envy, jealousy) and slander and evil speaking of every kind. Like newborn babies you should crave (thirst for, earnestly desire) the pure (unadulterated) spiritual milk, that by it you may be nurtured and grow into (completed) salvation. *I Peter 2:1,2.*

It is better to trust and take refuge in the Lord than to put confidence in man. *Psalms 118:8*

Believe in and on the Lord Jesus Christ - that is, give yourself up to Him, take yourself out of your own keeping and entrust yourself into His keeping, and you will be saved; (and this applies both to) you and your household as well. *Acts 16:31*

Now to Him Who, by and in consequence of the action of His power that is at work within us, is able to carry out His purpose and do superabundantly, far over and above all that we dare ask or think and infinitely beyond our highest prayers, desires, thoughts, hopes, or dreams. *Ephesians 3:20*

The Lord is near to all who call upon Him, to all who call upon Him sincerely and in truth. He will fulfill the desires of those who reverently and worshipfully fear Him; He also will hear their cry and will save them. *Psalms 145:18,19*

Cast your burden on the Lord, releasing the weight of it and He will sustain you; He will never allow the consistently righteous to be moved or made to slip, fall, or fail. *Psalms 55:22*

And my God will liberally supply (fill to the full) your every need according to His riches. *Philippians 3:19*

The poor and afflicted shall eat and be satisfied; they shall praise the Lord - they who diligently seek for, inquire of and for Him, and require Him as their greatest need. *Psalm 22:26*

Reflective Reassurance

I had to give God my problems and diseases and let Him figure them out. My job is to stay close to Him by meditating and studying His Word, continuing in prayer and surrounding myself with His people. Allowing Him to change me through circumstances and trials and trusting Him to do all things well is enough for me to handle. He's the Great Physician and I'm the submitting patient. Out of His care and away from His skillful hands, I will die. He has all the answers and knows all the treatments necessary for my well being. More accurately, He is my answer and He is my treatment. Knowing Him personally and intimately is the cure.

It has little to do with doing or not doing. It has everything to do with being – being in His presence. The power of His presence changes and enables us. When we are still and open before Him, we are transformed and made new. This is a lifetime journey – a continual daily maturing that advances regardless of evil to gain the prize of health and wholeness.

Chapter 9
I Need Somebody – Anybody! – To Love Me
Love: we'll give up everything to find it.

Just as I believed my parents did not love me, I believed no man could find me loveable. The lack of love I felt from my parents as a child is what I expected in my future relationships. I frequently debated whether to keep my boy friend who was emotionally abusive and disrespectful on dates. Each time a situation came up, I decided to stay with him. I saw myself as the person who could save him from his problems and make him into a wonderful husband. He would be so grateful to me for all I had done for him and our marriage would be perfect as we would be deeply in love with each other. I decided to marry him because I also knew no one else would have me and I better not miss my one chance to marry. Naturally, my marriage was a big disappointment. My husband never measured up to my expectations of what a husband and father should be. I was never able to trust my husband or feel free to be myself with him. The baggage I brought into the marriage from my childhood and schizophrenia strangled any possibility of making it work. He divorced me several years after the schizophrenia occurred again in my early thirties.

Not until after my husband left our family did I begin to make real efforts to gain self-control and strength. I had no one to lean on or make sure I was taken care of. He had been my strength and made the decisions. This created and fueled self-doubt and low self-esteem in me. The idea that I was not capable of being autonomous was a strong and clear message.

I have learned that trying to be responsible for another person is misguided love, at best. My son needed intervention so badly as a teenager after our divorce and I wanted to be the person that gave him the answers to his problems. I was telling him, in effect, that I believed he was not capable of handling things and that he did not have what it took to find his own solutions. My relationship with my son taught me that doing for him what he could do for himself was highly disrespectful. The more I made him feel dependent on me, the angrier he seemed to be. He continued to feel under my self-imposed power until I allowed him to be responsible for his actions and consequences.

To make sure I never ended up being unloved again, I tried to do everything for my husband who professed to love me. The sin in my marriage was an effort to keep my husband loving me. I couldn't lose his love. I had to have love. Anything, but not being rejected as unlovable again. I put up with disrespect, rudeness, emotional and physical abuse. There were always "good reasons" that my husband said or did that to my children or me. It was usually my fault. If I would have just done things better and not said certain things, he would have been wonderful and the greatest. I had a husband who loved me, that was all that mattered. That proved that I was a worthy and lovable person. Anybody who tried to tell me different just didn't understand or care about my family.

I accepted ill treatment because deep inside where I hid my past hurt and rejection, I knew I was not deserving of anything good. I had to hang on to my husband, for I believed no one else would consider having me. If others didn't harm me, I would harm myself through destructive relationships because I knew I was bad. I learned that, and learned it well, way back when, and will never forget.

I always made excuses for my son's behaviors. I believed all of his stories and bought into his every explanation. My daughter would become angry and lose patience with me, but it never changed the need I had to believe him. This particular weekend was no different. For six weekends, he was going to come put up a shed for me. At the last moment he would call and cancel. I put away any plans I might have for each weekend and defended each excuse he came up with. I would have put up with it sixteen weeks if he had asked me to. He did come at noon on the sixth Saturday and right away said he would be leaving the same afternoon. He left at 3:30 and the shed had barely been started. He spent more time traveling than he did with me. I was deeply hurt. It wasn't until Sunday that I began to cry and understand why I was hurt. This showed he didn't love me. Then a question popped in my head. Did I have to have his love? Did his love have to be shown me in this way? And the answer was no. The answer was no because I realized that he already loved me. His love for me and what he did were two separate things. He was acting self-centered and selfishly, but it had nothing to do with his love for me. It all had to do with what I believed. I had believed that I was unworthy of his love because of the things I had done and failed to do in his childhood. I was unlovable because I was bad. Yet I needed his love so badly and wanted it more than anything. What he did and said to me showed whether he loved me. When he promised to do something for me, that was evidence of his love. I let him go back on his word many times because I needed this demonstration of love no matter how long it took to get it. I couldn't believe that he ever lied to me because that would mean he didn't love me.

A young man with whom I worked closely was seen as one to be avoided because of his irritating and demanding behaviors. Taken from his parents at an early age, and in and out of foster homes all his life, he longed to be special and cared about.

He had no understanding of friendship, yet claimed to have friends wherever he went. It invariably turned out to be nothing more than a one-sided and often unwelcomed conversation with a sales clerk at some store. He carried a cell phone which was not activated. When around people, he would turn away and make the phone ring. Then he would answer it and carry on an impressive and detailed conversation with no one. He needed to feel cared about, so he created his own relationships by pushing himself on others or fabricating stories. He told himself this was real and meaningful. He had to lie to himself and others because the truth was too painful. Multiple sexual relationships gave him brief feelings of pleasure and being loved. He concocted lies upon lies to convince others how wonderful and capable he was, because he knew he was not. He couldn't admit doing any wrong because he might face rejection again. He looked for his happiness and approval in others and did not understand he had the power to choose his own feelings and actions. If others were made responsible for what happened to him, then he could avoid the pain of not measuring up and making mistakes. Because he did not choose, he was in the power of others, which either frustrated or pleased him. He had mood swings from elation to raging anger and rudeness depending on what others did or said to him. He was hurting deeply, but could not admit it. He could trust no one to handle his naked vulnerability with gentleness, kindness and a love that would stay no matter what. He was on a high-speed and destructive treadmill that never stopped or satisfied. It was easier for him to live a lie than live with the truth.

Like this young man, I was always thinking of how to get what I wanted and needed. I used people and said whatever was necessary to please them and look good. I drew attention to myself by bragging, talking about what I did, and even lying about things to sound better. I manipulated people to say positive things about me and made sure I got credit for things done right. I made excuses for mistakes and blamed others to protect myself from hurt and rejection. I did not want to be reminded of my worthlessness. To protect my self-image, I argued that I was right and the other person wrong. I had to build myself up to look good because I knew I wasn't. I prompted people to say good things about me and drew attention to myself. The more praise and credit I received, the more I required; for the well was always dry. Until I personally believed I was worthwhile and deserved good things, nothing or no one could satisfy my longings.

When I began looking for my first teaching job, I met with a career counselor to determine where I could apply in accordance with my interests and training. She pointed out to me that I had misspelled the word volunteer in my resume. I began telling her that my spelling was certainly right and that she was wrong. After strongly denying my mistake several times, I saw her look at me with a penetrating, knowing look. That silenced me. When home, I checked the dictionary and found that she was indeed correct. I was thoroughly embarrassed and ashamed.

Humbleness comes from looking at ourselves honestly. We are able to love ourselves and see the beauty in our own uniqueness. We are able to appreciate those special things about us that help us to serve others. We can even recognize that our once detested weaknesses are becoming strengths and are the very reasons we are able to do our chosen work so well. When we can love ourselves just the way we are, then it's not necessary to brag, manipulate or draw attention to ourselves. We are entirely content with the fullness of knowing that we are something beautiful and that our life does have purpose and meaning.

It was time for me to put the whip down. Time to silence the accusing tongue and cease the negative thoughts. I had to give myself permission to believe what God says about me. I had to give myself permission to love myself and forgive myself. Only I could move that mountain.

God didn't tell me to live a perfect life. He declared me perfect. This wasn't something I had to do. It's something He did. I asked Him to show me what I looked like through His eyes. The picture changed my life.

Affirmations From God's Word

Let not your minds and hearts faint; fear not, and do not tremble or be terrified and in dread because of them. For the Lord your God is He Who goes with you to fight for you against your enemies to save you. *Deuteronomy 20:3,4*

In returning to Me and resting in Me you shall be saved; in quietness and in trusting confidence shall be your strength. *Isaiah 30:15*

For from old no one has heard nor perceived by the ear, nor has the eye seen a God besides You, Who works and shows Himself active on behalf of him who earnestly waits for Him. *Isaiah 64:4*

The effect of righteousness will be peace internal and external, and the result of righteousness will be quietness and confident trust forever. *Isaiah 32:17*

Have you not heard? The everlasting God, the Lord, the Creator of the ends of the earth, does not faint or grow weary; there is no searching of His understanding. He gives power to the faint and weary, and to him who has no might He increases strength causing it to multiply and making it to abound. Even youths shall faint and be weary, and selected young men shall feebly stumble and fall exhausted; but those who wait for the Lord, who expect, look for, and hope in Him shall change and renew their strength and power; they shall lift their wings and mount up close to God as eagles mount up to the sun; they shall run and not be weary, they shall walk and not faint or become tired. *Isaiah 40:28-31*

Reflective Reassurance

The battles set before us in mental illness are many and life-long. The skirmishes seem endless and hit us from every direction. They are not ours to fight; God fights them for us. Our enemies are subdued as we hone the deadly weapons of faith, prayer, a righteous life, and God's Word.

Chapter 10
There's No Such Thing As Hopeless.
Never give up. I say again, never give up.

    Happiness was within my grasp. I had to let myself reach out and take it. I was in my mid-forties and was teaching kids that had emotional and behavioral problems. The job was affirming and brought out the best in me. I gained confidence and self-respect as my methods for working with the children were applauded. Medication was stable and was working. I still had bad days and weekends occasionally, but I was doing well. My focus and expectations began to change. It became clear that what I already had far out-weighed what I lacked. Recognizing the good in me and using that to build on began to make much more sense than concentrating on what I didn't have. What I believed about myself became more important than what someone said. Learning to love myself outweighed looking for what was wrong.

    Looking at my life as a spectator watching a game from a distance high in the stands helped me gain objectivity to my problems. I watched various scenes play out before me as a well-rehearsed production. It enabled me to see people and situations more clearly and opened the doorway to accept other explanations for why things happened the way they did. I had spent decades maintaining my Dad did not care about me. When he dug up thirty expensive flower bulbs for me, I explained that he was just tight with his money and wanted to keep me from spending money on something I could get free. With a friend's help, I realized for the first time that there could be a different reason. Maybe my perception of things was wrong. Perhaps it was an act of love.

Visualizing different parts of my life happening to a friend aroused compassion for myself. When struggling with critical inner thoughts toward myself, I would stop and ask, "What would I say to my friend if she told me this?" I could then counsel myself with mercy and kindness.

I had to appreciate my efforts to survive and have empathy for myself. I had to see that little girl of many years ago who did not feel loved and whose needs were not met, and cry for her. I had to have mercy on her and tell her that I knew she was powerless to have done anything different than what she did. I had to take the young person of years past, that thought she knew everything; and embrace her and tell her, "I forgive you for what you did and who you were. You didn't understand what you were doing or know the consequences." I've had to take the person I am today and give her the kiss of love and say, "It's OK. You did all that you knew to do at the time. If you could do it over, I know you'd do it different now. I know you would. And I forgive you and love you with all my heart."

I had expectations that I could realistically meet, when I dared to be average. When I had to be right all the time, it made me feel wrong all the time. Being worried continually about measuring up and comparing myself to others made me anxious and preoccupied with self. I decided to build myself up rather than beat myself up. It seemed more profitable to be in the construction business than the wrecking business. It took a lot of practice to talk kindly to myself, especially when I had messed up. Being my own worst enemy no longer seemed what God desired for me. My God-given uniqueness and His plan for my life became a reality. I now know my specialness does not depend on anyone else's opinion of me. And my opinion of myself never changes that fact either.

God had to have my help to resolve these problems. He couldn't do His part when I was working against Him. I hadn't been ready to receive and take care of what God wanted to entrust to me. When I was bitter, angry and fearful, evil had its hold on me. He had to get me prepared first. Accepting the pain, allowing myself to feel it, and then investigating it with God has been of fundamental importance in my growth toward health.

God so arranged my life that all props were gone. My marriage was ended and my children were emotionally estranged. My family was out of state. The job I went to college for was taken from me. Three friends turned their backs on me. It was me alone with God for the next ten years. I spent hours a day reading and rereading His word and it seemed I was always praying. I wanted nothing more than to spend time with God. He proved to be my perfect Counselor and my all-knowing Therapist.

Schizophrenia and depression are made up of a multitude of problems. These diseases had tentacles that reached out to every area of my life. God began the long process of dealing with each problem, one by one. Over and over again, He revealed things about me that needed to be changed. I would have a conversation with my Mom and immediately become angry about something she said or didn't say. I learned it wasn't her that needed to change, it was me. I demanded that she be perfect and meet every need I had just the way I wanted it met. It was the same way with my Dad. Every time I talked to them or visited with them, I was confronted with my inability to love them for who they were and not who I wanted them to be.

I was completely open to God and painfully honest. I held nothing back. When I became obsessed about something that I felt I did not do well enough, God helped me to see perfectionism as a hindrance and not an asset. It was always painful as I gave up cherished ways of thinking and had to embrace the new and unfamiliar. When one issue was worked through, it seemed another was right there needing to be confronted. I never dreaded this continual purging, for I knew that one more tentacle was losing its grip. As God helped me see my parents in a different light, I gained insight that had a positive ripple effect at work and in my children's lives. Many times I would slip back to the old ways and then I would understand anew why I must change. Suffering was my best teacher because my heart was open and willing to receive God's instruction.

It hurt to be confronted, and it was hard and painful to change. Pain was a motivator. Because I wanted relief, it sped up the process of healing and made me willing to accept help and look for answers. All that God did in my pain was redemptive. It was designed to bring me back to Him so He could have compassion on me and bless me. I did not understand how far I was from Him. Even as a forty-five year old woman, I still hated my Mom and Dad and believed all my problems were due to them. Spending time with God and in His Word, enabled me to see the bigger picture of my life.

Letting go of old ways and habits and finding the courage to venture into the new and unknown involves grieving. Part of me was dying. I was saying goodbye to the old thoughts, the automatic ways of responding and the history that fueled it all. Sometimes I even had to let relationships die in order to heal. I had to decide to not look back on all that was not for my spiritual edification. And that was hard; oh….so hard. It's a process that takes time and lots of little steps along the way. My triumphs were often small and many times unnoticed by others; but they were very real.

Until I began spending so much time with God, I saw perfectionism only as a strength in my life. The need to be perfect spurred me on and did not allow me to stop or give up or become satisfied. Without that tremendous drive in my life, I would have quickly whined in resignation to all the pain involved in turning my life around.

Choosing Godly friends who had the courage to speak from His Word, became a main avenue for God to reach me. I believe I would not have made it without my friends. God listens, touches, answers, challenges, comforts, and loves me through them. There have been times I know their words have been God's answer to a prayer.

Reading self-help books, both secular and Christian, was an unquenchable drive in my thirties and forties. I was searching for help, answers and guidance, and much was found. God has used the love of reading as a healing instrument in my life. Books that addressed the issues bothering me at the time seemed to jump out from a shelf or store display. About a year ago, I began to take an interest in other kinds of books too. It feels like a whole new world has been opened up for me.

Becoming aware of self-talk took tremendous effort. In the beginning, I did not notice the talking I did to myself inside my head. The putdowns and self-condemnation had become automatic and I believed they were deserved. When I started to slow it down enough to listen to it, I was somewhat shocked to hear what I was saying. I would never have spoken this way to my children, a friend or anyone. As I gained sympathy for myself, I was able to talk back to this negativity and say, "That is not true. I am not the scum of the earth. I have done some good things in my life. Just yesterday I let a lady go in front of me at the checkout lane." I started like this with little things. Most of the criticalness still went unchallenged, but I started. Once I got going, it became easier to stop the negativity often and quickly. Eventually the self-derision was replaced with empathy and kindness.

The fear of being the Antichrist was too real and entrenched to deal with in the same way. The voices swiftly took control when I attempted to talk back. God's Word was the weapon that worked.

When I was close to fifty years old, I was speaking to a Christian therapist about this fear and he asked if I believed Jesus was a man who once walked on this earth. I replied that I did. He then opened his Bible to 1 John 4:2 and read this to me: By this you may know (perceive and recognize) the Spirit of God: every spirit which acknowledges and confesses (the fact) that Jesus Christ (the Messiah) actually has become man and has come in the flesh is of God (has God for its source). I was not Satan's child. The spirit within me was not of him. Since then, I have found many verses that reiterate this truth. God's Word, spoken to this fear each time it seeks to confuse and terrorize me, renders it powerless.

Secular therapists were my mainstay for about twelve years. The good they did pales in comparison to God's therapy and the help of God's people. The world has some good answers; but it has no particular source of power that promises the ability to change us and do the impossible for us and through us.

The secular community will not tell which god is the true God for fear of being intolerant of other beliefs. Through tolerance training, people are encouraged to see the similarities in all religions and cultures. It appears there are few differences in the religions and one is as good as the other. While showing tolerance for all beliefs, the very things that have given Christianity its strength for thousands of years becomes lost. More lives are in bigger and bigger messes and more and more people are becoming casualties of ignorance and confusion as Christianity continues to be watered down.

Psychology has many labels for mankind's problems. The labels are all indicative of the varied ways we express our need for the true God and His truth. In *Telling the Truth to Troubled People*, William Backus, Ph.D., gives the spiritual prescription for anxiety disorders. "A child of God is in a most fortunate position. He has the Ruler of the entire universe for a Father. He doesn't lie, and He has promised that nothing can really harm His own. He has never promised that they won't experience rough times and unpleasant events, but He has guaranteed that not one of them can do real harm to His children. Moreover, He has promised to put limits on the testing so that it doesn't exceed what His child can bear." In depression, it is not uncommon for the sufferer to believe that God is angry with him and that his sins are too great to be forgiven. There also is no hope that God can love them again. Obsessive-compulsive disorders are centered on never being out of control and having the perfect solution for everything. Control of one's life must be given to God Who controls everything. Only God and His ways are perfect. It is impossible to trust God when one only trusts himself. The root of these problems and others go back to the spiritual by correcting mistruths with the truth of God and His Word.

The world offers very little truth that can be depended upon to be absolute and unchangeable. Man's thoughts change with the situation, the company that is kept, the individual's perspective and the different times we live in. However, consistency and predictability are what give us security and enable us to trust one another. When important fundamental beliefs for our life remain unchangeable and absolute, we can begin to build a life that gives us peace and rest for our minds and souls. The God of the Bible and His Word never change and they guide unerringly in every situation and problem. His Word guided me in accepting and understanding my inherent worth and value.

I could then begin doing things without the fear of failure immobilizing me. Even though I may fail or mess up, I can accept it gracefully because I know I am worthy no matter what I do. Failure no longer breaks me for it is not a done deal with God. He always gives me a second chance. As I started to make accomplishments, even small ones, I began to feel successful. Success bred success and doing hard things created self-esteem. I now know that I am capable and I can look at myself in a more positive light.

Doing things for others who cannot do for themselves, and not expecting anything in return, was one of the cornerstones for finding reasons to like myself. It took my mind off myself and put it on the needs of others. Doing loving things got me the love and attention I required so desperately. Whenever I gave with no strings attached, I received much more than I ever gave.

Volunteer work was a wonderful way to feel needed, valued and respected. One of the best things I did to help myself was to volunteer at our state revenue office one summer. Those ladies were so busy and overworked. They appreciated every little thing that I did and made a big deal out of my willingness to help. They put a picture of me on the front page of the newspaper taking driving license pictures! When the summer was over, I felt a foot taller and a whole lot better about myself. I felt good because I knew I had helped some deserving ladies and my efforts were deeply appreciated.

"Losing" my own life by helping and serving in another's life, I discovered surprisingly that I "found" my own life coming together and making sense like never before. It was in giving all away, so to speak, that I ended up finding everything I needed and desired. My self-centered eyes and thoughts were turned on someone else. I no longer dwelt so much on my own problems, hurts and pain. What I began to notice was that my pain was relieved, my problems seemed smaller and my hurts didn't hurt so much anymore. I believe God designed us to heal by giving ourselves away in love to others. I prospered and grew through serving others' needs. I shrivel up and die in many different ways when focused on me, myself and I.

The heart of God is people. When my focus is on God first and people second, I am where He wants me to be and my life becomes alive and exciting. I am no longer bored and discouraged; but have direction and a real sense of significance and importance for living.

When I started to understand that being "the best" and doing things perfectly was not required by God, I could relax and take the pressure off myself. I could begin to enjoy people and do unfamiliar things rather than feel fearful and frustrated. I could revel in being human, laugh at myself and have tolerance and compassion for others. I found that as an adult, I was the only one that required perfection of myself. It was only me that judged harshly and with no mercy.

It took a number of years for me to appreciate and feel comfortable with the middle ground and not the extremes. What behaviors are just part of the human condition and ones most people don't get upset over? How much excellence is enough and when does it become perfectionism? As I continue to work this out, I find myself relaxing and enjoying every area of my life like never before.

For many years after my divorce, I still slept on my side of the bed in a fetal position with my hands curled tight close to my face. I would not roll to the other side. In a sense, I was still hanging on to my past and the limitations of its pain. As I have become my own healthy and happy person, I find that I lay all over the bed in complete freedom and relaxation. Also noticeable is a new-found liberty to sing more loudly and with only one other person, rather than with only a large group. Mistakes are easily heard but no longer important to me. Giving myself permission to laugh frequently and with more abandon feels so good. Playful silliness and a sense of humor come more easily now, as I have come to love being me. My happiness, love of life and ease at being myself has been in direct proportion to my absence of guilt, shame and dislike of who I am.

God loved me before I knew Him, just the way I was. He didn't ask me to clean myself up to be good enough for Him. When I am trying and my heart is right, how and when I mess up is really beside the point with God. I am convinced that God will not ask me about the sins I've committed or how good I've been; but rather, how well and to what extent I have used and developed what He has given me.

He wants my heart. My heart, mind and soul become His as I spend time with Him and in His Word. The better I know Him, the more I love Him and desire to be with Him. The more I am with Him, the more I become like Him. I am changed simply by being in His presence. I did not change myself; I was changed by staying and dwelling with God Himself. God loves me regardless of what I do when my heart is submitted first to Him.

As awful as it was then, I realize now that I was in the best place to be. I had no one except God. My energies were poured into seeking Him and reading His Word. He was my only hope. There is nothing too hard, too twisted or too deep for God. And when there is nothing more important than God, a lot can happen.

Do you understand how blessed I am and that I am to be envied? I required God. No one else could help, for man had no answers. Seeking God with all of my heart was a necessity. I could not continue to live in chronic terror. There was no help to be found, so I would either die by ending my life or lose my mind completely. My physical body could not continue to handle the tremendous stress of fear. Even on medication, these problems did not diminish.

Medication only relieves symptoms. Relying solely on pills does not address the many issues that help to trigger the disease. They remain even while the medication is being effective. They continue to feed the disease and cause it to persist unabated. Working out the problems over time and with help will make it possible to take lower and lower doses of medication with better and better results. As I became healthier and stronger, the disease became weaker and less significant.

The schizophrenia, depression, divorce, and relationship to my parents guaranteed to make life difficult. The hidden gifts within these big troubles were not evident. Like an archeological dig, the treasures were hidden deep. I had to search until they were found – examining and putting the pieces together, unearthing the skeletons and learning from my history. Once the buried past was uncovered, it could be analyzed for authenticity and worth. Then I could embrace what was valuable and throw away what was refuse. There was much wealth to be found in the dark depths of disease.

My weaknesses are actually my greatest asset, because they have forced me to know God and to stay close to Him. So what appears to be so awful is really for my good. It has motivated understanding of my innermost self. I continued seeking, knocking and calling out until I found the new birthright God had been waiting for me to claim. Surrendering every area of my life to God's control and wisdom, I began exchanging my earthly birthright for God's birthright as His child. I exchanged depression for joy, terror for peace, fear for rest, anxiety for trust, hopelessness for God's perfect plans and confusion for a sound mind.

God is the Helper of all helpers and I was a ready vessel yearning to be filled with mental health. The severity of the cracks in my life allowed nothing to fill or soothe for long. I screamed for help, writhing in emotional pain that would not end. Therapy, medications, and other treatments simply offered temporary and superficial patches for my brokenness, because only God could replace my old wineskin with a new wineskin filled with the best wine.

I was given the earthly birthright of a broken mind, but what appeared to be a curse was turned into a blessing. What sought to destroy me, God has used as an asset in my work with troubled children and their families. Compassion and understanding well up inside when I see others grapple with the effects of mental illness. I have an insider's perspective on symptoms and ways to help while others may have only a textbook appreciation.

This disease has taken many people to places few have been and many only read or hear about. Overcoming the obstacles that abound in mental illness, helps forge a character of determination and strength. My journey from a nonfunctioning person to now is one that I am so glad I did not miss. I consider it a privileged experience.

If God is calling you to learn of Him by way of depression, schizophrenia, manic depression, panic attacks or any other mood or thought disorder, take His hand in yours and begin your travels with Him by your side, to a life you may have believed only "normal" people could have. "For He (God Himself) has said, I will not in any way fail you nor give you up nor leave you without support. I will not, I will not, I will not in any degree leave you helpless nor forsake nor let you down (relax My hold on you)! Assuredly not!" Hebrews 13:5.

Affirmations From God's Word

And you shall love the Lord your God with all your mind and heart and with your entire being and with all your might. And these words which I am commanding you this day shall be first in your own minds and hearts; then you shall whet and sharpen them so as to make them penetrate, and teach and impress them diligently upon the minds and hearts of your children, and shall talk of them when you sit in your house and when you walk by the way, and when you lie down and when you rise up. And you shall bind them as a sign upon your hand, and they shall be as frontlets or forehead bands between your eyes. And you shall write them upon the doorposts of your house and on your gates. *Deuteronomy 6:5-9*

But let him who glories glory in this: that He understands and knows Me (personally and practically, directly discerning and recognizing My character), that I am the Lord, Who practices loving-kindness, judgment, and righteousness in the earth, for in these things I delight, says the Lord. *Jeremiah 9:24*

It is good for me that I have been afflicted, that I might learn Your statues. *Psalm 119:71*

It is the Lord Who goes before you; He will (march) with you;

He will not fail you or let you go or forsake you; (let there be no cowardice or flinching, but) fear not, neither become broken (in spirit) (depressed, dismayed, and unnerved with alarm). *Deuteronomy 31:8*

I call heaven and earth to witness this day against you that I have set before you life and death, the blessings and the curses; therefore choose life, that you and your descendants may live and may love the Lord your God, obey His voice, and cling to Him. For He is your life and the length of your days. *Deuteronomy 30:19,20*

Reflective Reassurance

God has given me a life separate from the confines of mental illness. Because I know firsthand what life without God is like, I cling to Him for He is the source of all good things for today and all my remaining days. He is the beacon of light for all the darkness that mental illness brings. Confusion and fear create long, dark tunnels of despair and hopelessness. God's healing words can bring the brightness and clarity of noonday to dismal and deep emotional chasms.

Chapter 11
I'm Lonely, But Don't Ask Me To Do Anything About It.
Those incognito ogres: isolation and withdrawal

Loneliness and the desire to isolate myself are demons I wrestle with daily. It is so much easier not to get out and do things with others. The temptation and appeal to just stay at home and do my own thing easily overtakes me. But before long I realize that I'm a troubled person. I'm not happy. I only talk about myself. My mind becomes dull and depressed. I start beating myself up for not doing the things I know to do to take care of myself. The rut gets deeper as I feel worse and worse, and less energetic. I'm angry and disgusted with myself and soon find out I don't even want to get up in the morning. Daily hygiene becomes too difficult. I let the house go. I know what I should do but I don't do it. My knowing what to do and doing it can sometimes be very far apart. I don't answer phone messages for a few days. I call friends less frequently or not at all.

After joining a health club to get out and meet people, I became immobilized by fear of the unknown and the different. I paid my money for 3 months and went one time. There were no bad experiences but I never went back. After a friend and I went dancing at a singles group, I said it was great and really talked it up. My friend and I planned to go back and also to take dancing lessons. She called me twice to go back but I never went.

Even today it's still a constant battle to make myself do what is good for me. Doing what is not comfortable is hard. Leaving the familiar makes me sad and afraid. So instead, I do nothing. Sometimes

I decide to just forget it altogether. I decide not to put myself through all this. It's too upsetting. I come up with numerous and varied excuses.

> The stress of it all is too hard on my body.
> I know I can't do this.
> It's just my personality to stay at home and avoid people.
> My home is my only refuge and sanctuary. (escape?).
> I should be able to stay at home as much as I want and do the things I like to do.
> My work is demanding and stressful.
> I need to just be alone and do nothing or do just what I feel like doing.

When I'm quiet and even when I'm not, I can hear the small inner voice that encourages and prods me to do what is best for myself. My dear friends tell me again all they can to spur me on. It becomes a vicious cycle of not doing what I know I need to be doing and then beating myself up and feeling miserable. The fewer positive things I do, the more miserable and lethargic I become. On and on I go until one day I decide I've had enough. Self-induced suffering finally becomes repugnant.

When I do what I know to do, I'm so glad I did. I see again that the fears were ungrounded and that I made a big deal out of something that was not a big deal. And then, it's all over until the next time I have to do something out of my comfort zone.

It seems ridiculous. Will I ever learn that if I will just do the thing I fear I can avoid all the miserables? Will I ever catch on that it doesn't have to be hard and long and drawn out? I don't know. I hope so. But I do know one thing. God never leaves me. He never walks away in disgust. He's still there beside me reminding me that He's already given me everything I need and that He's prepared me for this. He never stops loving me even when I do the same stupid things over and over. Thank you, Jesus, for Your constant faithfulness that loves me the same regardless of what I do.

I know all the ways to avoid loneliness, and I know it's my choice to be lonely and isolated. I haven't resolved this obstacle in my life. It's still a very big challenge. Growth takes time and no one can do it for me. I have to do it myself but never by myself.

A recent scene from a dream demonstrates my struggle with withdrawal that is still very real. A lot of kids were in a play pit, soaring on ropes and swings and catching the next one while still in the air. There was lots of fun noise everywhere. I was seated on the floor next to the teacher. I began to slide under a low table to withdraw. I remember thinking, "I would never be free to do that and have fun."

Loneliness and withdrawal can be hard hurdles to master. Abraham Maslow has said that "The average person in the world does not have a true friend." The average person moves 14 times in his or her life. People everywhere are looking for warmth, kindness and friendship. If you provide warmth and kindness to others, it can be easy for friendship to follow. In relationships with other people, it is very important to remember, as Lucy Swindoll reminds us, "We can find something wrong with everything. (and everybody. This is my insert.) We have to choose to go with the positive or the negative."

God's Word instructs us to love our neighbor as ourself. This also seems to imply that we will love our neighbor as we love ourself. It is not possible to be full of hate and criticalness and still be able to give unconditional love and approval to our fellow man. We can give to others only what we have already given to ourselves. We see others through eyes that are colored either from the health or the disease of our own soul.

Each of us is unique in our emotional development just as we are in physical development. As toddlers, some of us walked later than others. Some of us learned to read before we went to school. Some of us struggled with reading all our lives. Others of us find math a mystery. For some of us, the math light bulb switches on as adults, even though the wattage may still be low.

The point is we all struggle. We all get miserable. We all do stupid things we said we'd never do again. The important thing is how we handle it. Do we give up in resignation? Do we walk away from it all with a feeling of failure? Or do we keep chipping away at our mountain? Do we refuse to give up, becoming determined to be better and better and thereby more useful in service for God's kingdom? Do we accept this as an opportunity and not a dead end?

God doesn't require us to be perfect in any way. He did that perfection thing for us a long time ago. He just asks that we never tire of working out our salvation and continue to grow and mature toward Christlikeness. It's never as hard as we think it will be for God is holding our hand and whispering loving encouragements in our ear continually as He meets all our needs in His perfect wisdom and timing.

No matter what label you've been given by a health professional, do not let it be an excuse for anything. When I read about the distinguishing characteristics of schizophrenia or depression, it is so easy to see everyone of them in my thinking and behavior. It becomes an explanation of why I do certain things or why I think in certain ways. And silently, but quickly, I assume the restrictions of the disease. I have found excuses to continue to act in the same hindering ways and facts to support why I cannot do anything different to help myself. When I dwell on and spend time on the negative features, I chain myself to certain behaviors. In a real sense, I am creating reasons for the symptoms to exhibit themselves for the first time or to continue and thrive. I am serving sickness by deferring to its supposed limitations and placing a very low ceiling on my expectations for growth and change. We are denying the power of God and doubting His promises to us. God raised up His Son and He will raise us up also.

Affirmations From God's Word

...work out (cultivate, carry out to the goal, and fully complete) your own salvation with reverence and awe and trembling (self-distrust, with serious caution, tenderness of conscience, watchfulness against temptation, timidly shrinking from whatever might offend God and discredit the name of Christ). Not in your own strength for it is God Who is all the while effectually at work in you and energizing and creating in you the power and desire, both to will and to work for His good pleasure and satisfaction and delight. *Philippians 2:12, 13*

For our light, momentary affliction (this slight distress of the passing hour) is ever more and more abundantly preparing and producing and achieving for us an everlasting weight of glory - beyond all measure, excessively surpassing all comparisons and all calculations, a vast and transcendent glory and blessedness never to cease! *2 Corinthians 4:17*

But you, beloved, build yourselves up founded on your most holy faith and make progress, rise like an edifice higher and higher, praying in the Holy Spirit; Guard and keep yourselves in the love of God. *Jude 20,21*

I am with you and will keep watch over you with care, take notice of you wherever you may go. *Genesis 28:15*

In the multitude of my (anxious) thoughts within me, Your comforts cheer and delight my soul! *Psalm 94:19*

Reflective Reassurance

We cannot overcome mental illness in our own strength. It can be too dark, deep and destructive for human intervention alone. We draw our power, wisdom and direction from God's inexhaustible supply. He is our teacher and the One Who changes our heart and renews our mind.

Chapter 12
One Last Try
Satan fights dirty and will hit below the belt.

What I like to call "Satan's last fling" took place when I was forty-eight years old and off medication by my choice. It was my desire to see if I could make it without medication. It seems like Satan gave it everything, in a last-ditch effort to do me in. Maybe he thought there would be no more chances to pull me under.

The intense battle in my mind lasted for about one week. Each night when dark approached, I became uneasy as the torment would begin. I slept very little. Wrestling with evil is the best way to describe those long and lonely nights. Fighting as hard as I knew how, I tried to resist the thoughts and ideas that led to believing I was the Antichrist. Countless times I cried, sweated profusely, tossed and turned, got in and out of bed and went from room to room. As the nights went by, I became more and more tired. It was harder to think clearly and I was physically drained of energy, as I was eating very little.

My daughter would come home from work, late at night, and prepare for bed and go off to sleep. In the bedroom next to her, I winced in fear and panic for what was happening to me. Then I would hear her again when she awoke and got ready for the day. Totally exhausted, I would still be cringing in fear and panic. Every night got harder. It seemed that I was being worn down.

The last night I heard what seemed to be Satan telling me that I was no longer going to be God's child. He was going to take Christ's spirit out of me and replace it with his spirit. I sat up on the edge of the bed in an effort to distract myself. Satan was there in front of me ready to do the deed. Numbly, and without the strength to resist anymore, I listened as he began. As he "took" God's spirit from me, he told me that I would be able to feel it leaving. And it "felt" like a vapor or shadow being pulled out. Then he placed his spirit in me which I also "felt". He ended by telling me he would put back everything so I would feel no different within myself. From all appearances, things would be like they had always been. Only he and I would know the truth.

When I laid back down, a whole series of thoughts paraded before me about a dear friend. She was really Mary, and her husband, Joseph; and others in her family were biblical characters also. It showed how recent happenings between my friend and me had been disguised and were actually spiritual episodes depicted in Jesus's life. These very same things would now be fulfilled in mine. I would be born from my friend after Satan's seed impregnated her. Jesus's life would be paralleled in mine through my friend and her family. Satan would be my father.

There were brief moments during this delusion that I was aware that this could not be true. It was somehow too ridiculous. Then I would be sucked back into it again. Body sensations of warmth and complete peace swelled within me while the scenes in my mind unfolded. Then it was all over. The hold on me seemed gone. I had lost ten pounds and was a physical washout.

Looking back on it now, I think Satan showed how determined and methodical he can be. He has knowledge of biblical fact; but, it is twisted, used in the wrong way and is designed wholly to deceive.

This all shook me for a while. But I was able to rise above it and see the error in it more clearly and quickly than ever before. In light of what God's Word really says, Satan made a complete fool of himself. For no one can pluck us from God's safe keeping. Once we belong to God, nothing and no one can change that.

When I finally understood Satan's intentions were literally to destroy and kill me, I became furious with him. I despised him and hated everything about him. He is so low, evil and crafty. He seeks to devour us by lying and trickery on any scale. I cannot stand him. He is absolutely and totally no good.

My trust in God's Word and what is true must be greater than my fears. Only my beliefs and self-talk can trigger the fears and only my beliefs and self-talk can stop the fears. I can choose to embrace truth or choose to embrace the fears and lies. I must choose the throne I want to stand at and worship. Will it be God's or Satan's? I need to speak and claim truth and recite Scripture without hesitation every time fear enters my mind. If I don't, each time it walks across my mind without correction it gains strength; for I am entertaining it. Entertaining one negative thought or lie leads to entertaining ten and then twenty and more. Before I know what has happened, I am controlled by fears that leave no room for reason or reality. Not one of them can be allowed to pass over the threshold of my mind. Truth, the beloved bouncer, must throw each one out every time without fail.

The Goliath of a schizophrenic is mental illness. It may seem we have no means of overcoming this giant. Darkness and despair cast their shadow across our entire life. Friends and family may say, "Have you seen what this disease has done to so many?" With David, we must say, " The Lord can deliver me out of the hand of this affliction." We pick up and use our meager competencies that are left intact while God honors our efforts in faith with victory. God will equip each one of us with all that we require to be giant killers. He is waiting for you to ask for what you need for He longs to give you His best.

Affirmations From God's Word

Sin crouches at your door; its desire is for you, but you must master it. *Genesis 4:7*

Do not let yourself be overcome by evil, but overcome and master evil with good. *Romans 13:21*

For the Spirit which you have now received is not a spirit of slavery to put you once more in bondage to fear, but you have received the Spirit of adoption producing sonship in the bliss of which we cry, Abba Father! *Romans 8:15*

Now to Him Who is able to keep you without stumbling or slipping or falling, and to present you unblemished and blameless and faultless before the presence of His glory in triumphant joy and exultation with unspeakable, ecstatic delight. *Jude 24*

May grace (God's favor) and peace (which is perfect well-being, all necessary good, all spiritual prosperity, and freedom from fears and agitating passions and moral conflicts) be multiplied to you in (the full, personal, precise and correct) knowledge of God and of Jesus our Lord. *II Peter 1:2*

Keep on asking and it will be given you; keep on seeking and you will find; keep on knocking (reverently) and (the door) will be opened to you. *Matthew 7:7*

Reflective Reassurance

No matter how bad it gets, keep on. God is faithful.

Chapter 13
But If I'm Not Healed, Something Is Wrong.
Can this too be healing?

    I had asked God to heal me. Again and again, I cried out to God to completely take away the schizophrenia and depression. Again and again, I had prayed to be normal. Being normal was my greatest desire. For many years, it seemed the ears of God were deaf.

    God began revealing errors in thinking about my healing. One error was that my reason for wanting to be completely well was perfectionism. Measuring up and being the best meant getting free of disease. My value as a person was tied up with succeeding in this area. It was about getting free of the disease so that I could show that I was the best at getting well. This would prove that I was special and would bring me attention and recognition. If this healing did not take place, then I was lacking and there was fault in me. The continuation of the mental disorder was a sign of my weakness; therefore, I had to overcome it. This attitude enabled me to fight and not give up. It made me stubborn and determined that I would succeed. When someone was negative about my prognosis, I bulldoggedly dug in to show him or her wrong. Doing things that couldn't be done, so to speak, would prove my worthiness.

    It was so hard to give up the need to be healed. Stopping the medication or missing doses became a way of checking my progress in beating the schizophrenia and later the depression. Tremendous disappointment overshadowed everything when symptoms clearly came back each time. My healing was self-centered and self-serving and therefore not for my best good. I wanted to get the credit for curing myself rather than God.

In mental illness, there is never one problem to be addressed, but many. My children were angry and hated me. Unforgiveness and negativity toward my ex-husband and parents ruled my spirit. Suspicion and distrust were natural ways of thinking. Socially, I was in need of companionship. My people skills were not developed well and I was still uncomfortable in most group situations. I had to have control of myself and my circumstances at all times. The list could go on and on. These attributes stoked the fires of schizophrenia and depression. Physical healing is only part of the picture.

To be useful and worth anything in this world, I believed I had to be physically well. If I completely lost my physical health or if I never had it the way I thought I should, it meant my life was doomed to a lonely and meaningless existence. If I could not be healed, by my own efforts or with God's help and intervention, then I had nothing and could be nothing. Schizophrenia pointed its nasty finger at my lack of faith and certainly my lack of strength and character in not being able to overcome. It spotlighted to me again my inability to measure up and my failure in my relationship with Jesus Christ. I was lacking; therefore, I was not healed.

Physical healing may come as a by-product of spiritual and emotional healing. It may be the result in a long process of the healing of the mind and soul. In my shortsightedness, I lived and thought like this life here on earth was everything. Even when I admitted it was not, I found it hard to let go of almost everything that I considered essential in this life. Things like my home, car, work and my children were more important to me than heavenly things. My grasp on the value and significance of eternal things was sometimes very weak. I truly did not understand there was no comparison between earthly treasures and heavenly treasures. They are so far apart, they cannot even be considered as having anything in common. I had to accept that complete physical healing may be something that is considered unnecessary or not for my highest good by God's 20/20 vision into my future. I had to let God be God and I had to give up my control and surrender to Him.

I forgot that others were touched by my illness. My problems were never just about me. I was surrounded by on-lookers on every side that were part of my good days and bad days, my illness and my healing, the worst and the best. They were also benefactors of my experiences and my growth toward wholeness and holiness. My sickness may be the very means by which others see Christ, as by God's power I am able to rise above my circumstances and continue on. Others may gain hope, strength, reassurance, and determination when they watch me meaningfully survive. When I continue to stand in praise and live joyfully, in spite of obstacles, I am working out a purpose much greater than myself. Treasures are being accumulated that are out of this world in value and everlasting significance. When I believed my life impacted the lives of others, it brought some sense to the confusion I so often felt and gave me reason to not give up.

It is a myth that limitations equals uselessness. God was eagerly awaiting permission to turn my weaknesses into strengths. He turned water into the best wine. God could take my broken and sick past and create a future of beautiful design that blessed me with the very desires of my heart that I believed could never be mine. Limitations were only opportunities for God to display all of who He is and all that He promises me of Himself. God was full of treats for me…and not tricks. My infirmities give me reasons to search God out and reasons to try Him, prove Him and trust Him. If I could have handled everything in my life and things always went my way, I would have never had a need for God. It was when life was out of my control and everything seemed to be going wrong that I required and called out to God. What was best for me centered on eternal issues and blessings and not just on what pleased me and fit into my plans. Divorce and disease may have been the only way to break through my stubbornness and pride and get my attention on spiritual matters. If I believe that spiritual matters are far more important than physical matters, then I can see the need and the value of my infirmities. When thinking about the length of eternity, my life on earth is maybe comparable to fifteen minutes. Spending forty-five years of my life finding God and getting my life in order doesn't seem so bad when comparing it to a few minutes of eternity. What really is important is that I did it and that I know where my eternity will be spent. I can't fully understand life everlasting but God does. He knows I cannot even visualize in my wildest dreams what heaven will be like. Therefore, He did whatever necessary to make sure I did not miss eternity with Him. Suffering is temporary. My soul's condition will be permanent for an eternity. I didn't want to miss any of what God has for me in heaven, so He had my permission to do whatever it took to get me ready.

I began to go through an important change. I had to cling tighter to God than I clung to wanting health. Having an intimate and personal relationship with God became more important than what He could do for me physically. I began to see that many things were more important than whether I had healing. It was more important for me to trust God enough to let Him decide whether I was completely healed. If the disease remained acute and I spent my life confined to a hospital, it was of greater consequence to trust God's ability to care perfectly for my children emotionally, spiritually and physically. I needed to know God's character so well that I did not doubt His knowing best even if that meant I was in a catatonic state for years and my children forgot about me. I had to believe that even if the worst case scenario of schizophrenia happened, God was in charge and He loved my children and me and was working out His best for us. Learning to lay my life in the arms of Jesus and say, "Whatever, Lord," transformed my greatest fears to quiet peace.

The more I found out about God in the midst of my suffering, the more I realize that suffering can be the vehicle that enables me to learn of God and His character in ways otherwise impossible. Learning about God in this way has prepared me to accept other discomforts more easily. It has brought health to my sick soul because my attitude is realistic and my mind is open. It would have been easy to misplace my energies and emphasis. Visiting different doctors, changing medications, trying new therapists, attending workshops and looking to the latest research certainly have their time and place.

My time needed to be invested with God and His truth and then all these other areas would naturally fall into place. When I learned to seek God and keep on seeking Him, needed answers become by-products of learning about Him. I did not seek so that I could get what I want. I was seeking to get God. For when I was focusing on God and not on my suffering, I had everything I needed and desired. Suffering can be welcomed as my friend, teacher and conduit to God; rather than my enemy.

When my prayers are not answered the way I want them to be, I need to look at myself. God is probably waiting on me. He is usually having to prepare me in some way before He can answer. God is not a machine that dispenses blessings at my request. If God should give me everything I ask, I would have little reason to depend and rely on Him to meet my needs. There would be little motivation to come to know His ways and thoughts personally and intimately.

He is an all-knowing, all-loving, all-powerful, all wise, all-everything God whose thoughts and ways are high above mine. They are much greater and deeper than mine could ever be. Yet I have argued and insisted on my way and in my time. Like I know what is best! How arrogant and prideful! How ignorant and small I really am! All I can say to a God so great and awesome is, "Here I am. Do with me as You in your wisdom see fit. Use me for Your honor and glory. Let my desires be Your desires because I am nothing compared to You." To quote Blaise Pascal, "Let me no longer wish for health or life, but to spend it and end it for You, with You, and in You. I pray neither for health nor sickness, life nor death. Rather I pray that You will dispose of my health, my sickness, my life, my death, as for Your glory."

My life must be devoted to God rather than to the healing of my life. Pain and suffering have been a sure and quick route to God, it seems. It is not good for my eyes to be focused on the symptoms of my condition; but rather on the growth that resulted. God is interested in healing my mind and heart so that my soul is healthy. My soul has always been God's priority.

Medication is not negotiable for me. In my own strength, I am nothing. "My strength and power are made perfect (fulfilled and completed) and show themselves most effective in your weakness." II Corinthians 12:9 For the present and especially the uncertain future, I have to trust God that I will always be able to get and afford the medication. Meeting my needs is God's business.

Some say that medication for emotional problems is just a crutch. Well, I say, "Thank you, God, for crutches!" A crutch enables a person to move about, do the normal activities of a day and continue with life. Without a crutch, a person might be bedridden, home bound and unable to work. Life would be very limited. Similarly, medication for emotional problems enables us to do things we could not do and to think in ways we could not think otherwise. Medications relieve anxiety, anger and depression so that we have the ability to start working on our problems and finding solutions. While using a crutch for an injured leg or foot, we may require physical therapy to strengthen and help heal the injured muscle or bone. When using a mental crutch, we may also get therapy to strengthen emotionally weak areas such as self-esteem or relationships. We all require supports of some sort to help us cope and continue in spite of our human frailties and limitations. Medications and therapy can be part of God's answer and help for us.

Affirmations From God's Word

Faithful is He Who is calling you to Himself and utterly trustworthy, and He will also do it and fulfill His call by hallowing and keeping you. *I Thessalonians 5:24*

Seek, inquire for, and require the Lord while He may be found claiming Him by necessity and by right; call upon Him while He is near. Let the wicked forsake his way and the unrighteous man his thoughts; and let him return to the Lord, and He will have love, pity, and mercy for him, and to our God, for He will multiply to him His abundant pardon. *Isaiah 55:6.7*

Do not earnestly remember the former things; neither consider the things of old. Behold, I am doing a new thing! Now it springs forth; do you not perceive and know it and will you not give heed to it? I will even make a way in the wilderness and rivers in the desert. *Isaiah 45:18,19*

He who heeds instruction and correction is not only himself in the way of life but also is a way of life for others. *Proverbs 10:17*

Seek, aim at and strive after first of all His kingdom and His righteousness (His way of doing and being right), and then all these things taken together will be given you besides. *Matthew 6:33*

Thus says the Lord: Stand by the roads and look; and ask for the eternal paths, where the good, old way is; then walk in it, and you will find rest for your souls. *Jeremiah 6:16*

May God's peace be yours, that tranquil state of a soul assured of its salvation through Christ, and so fearing nothing from God and being content with its earthly lot of whatever sort that is, that peace which transcends all understanding shall garrison and mount guard over your hearts and minds in Christ Jesus. *Philippians 4:7*

I the Lord will instruct you and teach you in the way you should go; I will counsel you with My eye upon you. *Psalms 32:8*

Reflective Reassurance

Medication is God's gift to me. Although this fallen and sin-filled world can be blamed for this disease, God reaches down to me with the means to rise above it. Yes, it never seems fair to have any debilitating disease, but even here, God made a way.

Chapter 14
How Great Are Your Mercies Toward Us!
The gift of two dreams

Two dreams, in particular, brought hope and a conviction that there would be an eventual end to the relentless fear that tormented me without mercy.

In the first dream, I was standing in the middle of my house. The walls of the house were very low, about the height of an adult's knees. I could see everything on the outside of my house clearly. While standing there, I saw a man walk purposely toward my house. I recognized him immediately as Satan. He was a small, hard looking man who appeared old and toughened for his age. Without pausing to check, but knowing perfectly, he walked straight to the part of my wall that had a crack in it. I was not aware that the crack was there, but he knew. His lower body assumed the shape of the crack and his upper torso remained unchanged as he purposely came into my house and began to touch everything. Nothing was left untouched. He opened every cabinet door and every drawer. Each thing in them, he would pick up, look at intently, and then put back in its place to look as if it had never been touched. I stood silently and watched until he was finished, and then I firmly said, "Satan, get out of my house!" And he immediately left.

This dream gave tremendous hope. After reading some about the symbols in dreams, I learned a person's house in a dream is usually their mind. The dream let me know that there would be an end to Satan's affliction. Satan, it seemed, knew my weak area and entered there. It also told me that I had the power to tell him to leave and he would. Satan only did what I allowed him to do.

From then on, I tried telling him to leave as I had in the dream. I spoke firmly and loudly and in the name of Jesus. I begged and pleaded with God to put him in chains so he would leave me alone. Discouragement set in because the thoughts and fears soon began to return. But I began learning that I did have control over my thoughts and that it would be an on-going battle against years of entrenched habits that resisted change. Persistence and alertness became the keys to controlling what I allowed my mind to think.

The second dream involved my Dad. He stood below me while I watched him feverishly build a structure of wood. There was no beauty or sense to what he was making. It was without any form and made haphazardly from scrap pieces of wood. He asked me to hold up something that looked like a 4x8 piece of plywood. It was attached to the top of what he was building. It appeared to protect him from the bright sun while he worked. While I was holding it, it slipped out of my fingers. As it fell down, the edge hit my sister on the head. She was bleeding and I picked her up and began to carry her. At this time, my sister was large and there was no way I could ever lift or carry her. But, in my dream I carried her a long distance. Eventually, I had to lay her down. I cradled her head in my lap and watched her as she died in my arms. Her face depicted stages of death. It first became very pale and then white. It began wrinkling and drawing up. Then it finally dried up in death. While I held her, a med-flight helicopter circled in the distance, surveying the scene, but never landed.

At first, this dream made no sense, even though I tried to figure out it's meaning. Sometime later, I awoke during the night and knew the meaning of the dream: The dream depicted my Dad, in a frenzy, building a confused structure with me "helping" him while he worked. There were unhealthy and destructive beliefs in our family that created confusion and disorder, and made little sense in light of reality. My life reflected this disordered and confused thinking, and in effect, supported my family's unhealthiness (the holding up of the 4x8 board) by living out these thinking errors and passing them on to my children. Dropping it meant that I had let my Dad down by disappointing him and not measuring up to his expectations, especially in my marriage. The board hit my sister's head, which showed that the unhealthiness had affected or injured my mind. Carrying my large sister was the burden of the Antichrist fear. It was a load impossible for me to carry, but one that I carried for many years. The load was put down finally and the fear died in stages, or over a period of time. Therapists and hospitals had been in my life; but in hindsight, it seems they observed behaviors and symptoms; but like the helicopter did not really help. Understanding this dream brought such immediate peace and comfort that I just burst into tears. The clock showed a few minutes after one in the morning, which reminded me of the verse in Psalms that speaks of joy coming in the morning. It seemed my morning had come, and I cried some more.

The Crack in the Wall

No matter what the problem area of our life is (what shape or size the crack), Satan can adjust to it and work his way in without any difficulty. If we allow him, he will touch everything in our life and spirit and mind. He will leave nothing untouched whether it is big or small. He intends to rob, kill and destroy; but he can only do to us what we allow him to do. Satan is God's footstool and will one day bow down to God. He is only free to do what he has permission from God to do. He is little and God is great big. He comes to take away while God comes to heal and restore. Satan lies; but God speaks truth. God is life and Satan is death. We must choose who we want to serve, for one of them will be our master.

The key to winning any battle is to know your enemy. Satan wants to be worshipped and deified like God. He wants us to deny our Savior and he wants to destroy God's people, the saints. He works unceasingly to delude, confuse and wear down people. He labors furiously to cause people to blame, mock and curse God. He promises everything for little or nothing, but gives nothing at the cost of everything. He is already defeated, for Jesus defeated sin and death. He will one day fall down and acknowledge God and spend eternity in the depths of hell. The only power he has over us is what we give him. The sinful world and Satan has no power over us for Christ defeated both. Our faith doesn't live by our circumstances, by explanation or by appearances. It lives by the reliability of God's Word. Ask God to open your eyes and soften your heart to see and believe these things. Let Him renew your mind into all truth.

God gives us everything we need to make it, whether it be friends, literature, music, tapes, dreams to encourage and enlighten, messages on radio and TV, or speaking to us through His Word, His Spirit and His servants. When we have Him, we have everything. He supplies it all.

Affirmations From God's Word

...for I knew that You are a gracious God and merciful, slow to anger and of great kindness, and (when sinners turn to You and meet Your conditions) You revoke the (sentence of) evil against them. *Jonah 4:2*

I have told you these things so that in Me you may have perfect peace and confidence. In the world you have tribulation and trials and distress and frustration; but be of good cheer and take courage; be confident, certain, and undaunted! For I have overcome the world. I have deprived it of power to harm you and have conquered it for you. *John 16:33*

...For He is not weak and feeble in dealing with you, but is a mighty power within you. II *Corinthians 13:3*

And I am convinced and sure of this very thing, that He Who began a good work in you will continue until the day of Jesus Christ

-- right up to the time of His return -- developing that good work and perfecting and bringing it to full completion in you. *Philippians 1:29*

Come to Me, all you who labor and are heavy-laden and overburdened, and I will cause you to rest, and I will ease and relieve and refresh your souls. Take my yoke upon you and learn of Me, for I am gentle (meek) and humble (lowly) in heart, and you will find rest and relief and ease and refreshment and recreation and blessed quiet for your souls. For my yoke is wholesome and useful, good - not harsh, hard, sharp, or pressing, but comfortable, gracious, and pleasant, and My burden is light and easy to be borne. *Matthew 11:28-30*

I sought (inquired of) the Lord and required Him (of necessity and on the authority of His Word), and He heard me, and delivered me from all my fears. *Psalm 34:4*

Light arises in the darkness for the upright, gracious, compassionate, and just (who are in right standing with God). *Psalm 112:4*

Weeping may endure for a night, but joy comes in the morning. *Psalm 30:5*

In conclusion, be strong in the Lord - be empowered through your union with Him; draw your strength from Him - that strength which His boundless might provides. Put on God's whole armor - the armor of a heavy-armed soldier, which God supplies - that you may be able successfully to stand up against all the strategies and the deceits of the devil. *Ephesians 6: 10,11*

Reflective Reassurance

God makes the way through any problem possible for us. He devises a completely unique plan of release for each of us. We just have to be willing to let Him work it out in our life on His timetable and according to His conditions. We must be the soft, pliable clay on the Potter's wheel. In the end, His plan always honors Himself and gives us the desires of our heart.

Chapter 15
I'm in Control. I Can Handle This by Myself.
Only God is self-sufficient.

At the suggestion of my first therapist, I decided to go back to college. I had accumulated about thirty hours in the fourteen years since high school. My day would be filled with meaningful activities that would distract my obsessive thinking. This was a big step for a person with almost no confidence. But it appealed to my love of learning, writing and reading.

During my freshman English class, I had to be able to pass a writing proficiency test in order to go on with my studies and to graduate. No grades were given; it was a pass or fail test. My hopes and expectations were sky high as I knew this would be easy to pass. It made me a little nervous not knowing the subject matter until the time of the test. But feeling that I could handle it, I was ready to demonstrate my abilities in writing. This was an area of my life in which a glimmer of self-assurance and capability occasionally flickered.

The different subject areas were listed on the board. Choosing the one I was most comfortable with presented little problem. I began to write easily and quickly. I was motivated by knowing that this would be a cinch for me as I continued to write with little effort. The test ended and I confidently turned in my writing, ready for it to be graded by various English faculty members. In high school, English classes were probably my favorite; and it seemed no different now.

Several weeks later, the professor announced the results to the class. There were only three students who failed, and I was one of them. I was devastated. The little self-assurance that had remained was ripped from my sensitive spirit. Now I knew that even this area that I still held onto with some pride was also a big joke. There was nothing good about me. I didn't know anything. How dare I think that I could be capable in some way! Everyone and everything in my world that had shown me to have no worth was absolutely right.

As I left class, I felt nauseated. For the next four days I threw up and could keep nothing on my stomach. My husband took me to the emergency room where I was admitted. The on-duty doctor suspected gall bladder problems.

For two days I continued to throw up, in spite of the anti-nausea injections I was given regularly. My family doctor asked what had happened before I was admitted and I told him about failing the test. It was dinnertime at the hospital and my doctor told the nurse to bring me a tray. He said simply, "You are ready to eat now and you will be able to keep it down." I couldn't figure out why he said that, for I was still sick to my stomach. He knew I couldn't hold anything down. But as I thought about what he had said, I decided that maybe he was right. Maybe he knew something I did not know. I ate dinner that evening and did not throw up again. I went home the next day doing fine.

In two weeks, the three of us that had failed would take the test one more time. If we failed again, we would need remediation classes to continue our education. The English professor said she did not understand why I had failed. She stated my writing was good and she was sure I would pass this next time. There was nothing she could have said that would change the way I felt. The facts were there. I had failed and that was all that mattered. The professors had seen something I hadn't seen; and they were the experts. They knew good writing when they saw it; and mine was a failure.

The time for the second test came. The subjects were put on the board. I felt I knew absolutely nothing. My mind was frozen, a complete blank. I sat in paralyzing fear, with a knowing my writing was no good. I couldn't do it. There was nothing I could write, for I believed I was a nothing.

    The professor came up to me and asked what was wrong. Weakly, I said that I couldn't do it. I didn't know how to write. She encouraged me, "Yes, you can do this. You are a good writer." I continued to sit there just frozen in time. She came back again and said, "You can do this. Start by listing the main ideas you want to talk about, and then list other ideas under them."

    I said, "I can't do it. I can't write. Nothing will come."

    When time was called, I maybe had five words on my paper. She proceeded to write about four main topics down for me and then wrote developing ideas under them. She said again that I could do this, and to take my paper and go to the top floor of the library where it was quiet. I was to use as much of the remaining afternoon as I needed to finish what she had started for me. Then I was to take it to her office and place it face down on her desk. As I thanked her, she assured me again that I could do this and do it well.

    This time I passed. How, I don't know. The writing sample was short; and it seemed choppy and not developed like the first. I wasn't in control this second time. God made everything fall into place for me to pass. I did not depend on what I could do. I had been stripped of everything -- stubbornness, pride, self-sufficiency and self-esteem. God wants us to rely on Him for all that we do. We are to believe in His greatness and not ours. It is not our abilities and strengths that get us through anything; but, God working in us and through us infusing us with all that we require. We are to depend on God and not ourselves. He takes, so that He can give back in a way that declares He is our All in All. He wants to be our answer, our hope and our sufficiency. We are made in His likeness and for His glory, and no one else's.

Affirmations from God's Word

    My grace and My favor and loving-kindness and mercy is enough for you and sufficient against any danger and enables you to bear the trouble manfully; for My strength and power are made perfect and fulfilled and completed and show themselves most effective in your weakness. Therefore, I will all the more gladly glory in my weaknesses and infirmities, that the strength and power of Christ the Messiah may rest yes, may pitch a tent over and dwell upon me! So for the sake of Christ, I am well pleased and take pleasure in infirmities, insults, hardships, persecutions, perplexities, and distresses; for when I am weak in human strength, then I am truly strong, able, powerful in divine strength. *II Corinthians 12:9,10*

And after you have suffered for a little while, the God of all grace - Who imparts all blessing and favor - Who has called you to His own eternal glory in Christ Jesus, will Himself complete and make you what you ought to be, establish and ground you securely, and strengthen and settle you. *I Peter 5:10*

Lean on, trust in, and be confident in the Lord with all your heart and mind and do not rely on your own insight or understanding. In all your ways acknowledge Him, and He will direct and make straight and plain your paths. *Proverbs 3:5,6*

I have strength for all things in Christ Who empowers me - I am ready for anything and equal to anything through Him Who infuses inner strength into me; that is, I am self-sufficient in Christ's sufficiency. *Philippians 3:13*

And He humbled you and allowed you to hunger and fed you with manna, which you did not know nor did your fathers know, that He might make you recognize and personally know that man does not live by bread only, but man lives by every word that proceeds out of the mouth of the Lord. *Deuteronomy 8:3*

For God did not give us a spirit of timidity - of cowardice, of craven and cringing and fawning fear - but He has given us a spirit of power and of love and of calm and well-balanced mind and discipline and self-control. *II Timothy 1:7*

Reflective Reassurance

It is not self-confidence that we require, but God-confidence. He promises to empower us with all that we need for any circumstance. It doesn't matter how incapable we may feel, for God is entirely capable. We draw everything we need from His endless supply. We must take what He says to us and believe it to be true. This is called faith.

Chapter 16
Losing It All Again
God's Plans are the Best

There was way too much going on inside my head that would not allow me to relax and immerse myself fully into the love of academic learning. A light schedule of classes was required, as my level of concentration remained poor. Understanding the material and appreciating how it all came together in the classroom escaped me. I continued to skim the surface and did not comprehend the meaning or usefulness of much. Memorizing for tests was my way of getting through school. Black and white thinking made it impossible to learn a foreign language or grasp abstract math ideas. Anything different from the way I thought was incomprehensible. There was no room for new ideas to fit into my concrete experience.

Six years after I started college full-time and at the age of 39, I graduated with a 3.2 grade point and was a member of the educational sorority for excellence in scholarship. I was appointed to a position teaching first grade in public school one month after graduation.

What a hard first year! My hang-ups were the biggest problem. I believed I could be everybody's answer to prayer. If I worked long enough and hard enough, I could fix every child's problem and maybe even show parents the errors of their ways. What a burden! How frustrating and upset I always felt! I never thought I did enough and nothing was good enough. Things had to be a certain way or they were no good and wouldn't work.

Getting out of my own way has been my biggest obstacle in

learning to teach well. I have probably learned more from my students than any child learned from me. I am so thankful that growth and learning are not reserved only for the young. My seven years were exemplary as I was responsible, dependable and took my job seriously. I loved first grade and loved teaching. I went above and beyond the requirements of my position.

At the start of the school year, certain teachers wanted different reading curriculum; but I verbally supported what I and another teacher had been using quite successfully for the past three years. I became a threat to the other teachers and was labeled a troublemaker. But this one time, what I believed was best for the children outweighed my doormat personality. So I did express my concerns about the change in curriculum, although I went ahead and made the change, and used it in my classroom throughout the year. My concern was determined to be insubordination and I don't believe I could have done anything to change that opinion. It seemed to be something they wanted to believe about me.

After the problems began in September, two friends and I met almost daily after school to pray. We continued to pray up to the school board meeting in the spring. Our prayers focused on our desire for God to expose the wrongdoing and the people that appeared to target me. It seemed our prayers were not heard. This was more evidence to me of my guilt and that the label of troublemaker was correct. Evaluations and situations during the school year were so ordered and perceived that I did indeed appear to be a big problem.

We got in touch with a Christian lawyer who was reported to defend teachers who were wronged and had no financial resources. The lawyer took my case and we had a hearing before the school board. Their decision remained the same.

The school board voted on my dismissal in June, at the end of the school year. The meeting was announced twenty-four hours in advance. Over 100 signatures were gathered in those twenty-four hours for a petition in my support. The meeting was moved from the library to the cafeteria as the community arrived. A dear friend sang the song, "I Can Begin Again," by Larnell Harris and dedicated it to me. The school board voted unanimously not to rehire me and not to consider the wishes of the 100 petitioners. Friends encouraged me to go to court. The verdict again remained unchanged. It was a most difficult time. I was single and without a job. As a teacher, my career seemed finished.

Was I insubordinate like they said? I didn't know what was right. I was confused and struggled to defend my good intentions in conversations with the principal and superintendent. I truthfully denied I was a troublemaker but I had been declared the problem in childhood, and then in my marriage and here once again I was the problem. Was I insubordinate? My children said I was the problem in their life and now some of my fellow teachers, principal, superintendent and school board said it too.

This was a time of extreme worry, anxiety, doubt and fear. I felt totally out of control. My world was spinning wildly with a loss of all direction and purpose. Again I was being stripped of everything I took pride in. I began to believe what they said about me was true. I wasn't the good person and teacher that I thought. My good work of the past seven years was just a cruel misconception on my part. What I thought had been honorable behavior was perceived as dishonorable and a problem to be gotten rid of quickly. My self-esteem spiraled downward. There really was no good in me. Everything I attempted was no good. I was not the person I thought I was but was obviously vile.

Global and obsessive thinking consumed me. Failure and the rejection of others surrounded me on every side for as long as I could remember. I had to be guilty because of all that was happening. I knew I was the worst person who ever walked the face of the earth. Being fired verified everything bad I had ever believed about myself. It fit perfectly into the scheme of my past. I began to contemplate suicide. It would have been very easy to cave in to it all. With no reason to doubt my lack of goodness and value, I could just give up and die. Except for some people who told me it wasn't so. Thank you, God, for those people. They gave me something to hold on to when there was nothing else. They helped me to consider another side to the story of me that I had not considered before.

A watchdog group of sorts was formed in response to my situation. We met once a month in an effort to expose any further problems at the school and to encourage patrons to be involved and aware of school issues. It was a wonderful time of fellowship and united purpose. These people believed in and supported me. They trusted my character and had faith in my goodness and motivation to give the children what worked. They assumed my innocence rather than assuming my guilt. They saw good in me and spoke of me with admiration and not condemnation. They were an antidote to offset and challenge my old belief system that had me in chains and shackles. Their persistent encouragement and unwavering verification of my value and worth laid the foundation for the emergence of a new and much kinder view of myself.

Two friends wanted to start a private Christian school to offer an alternative to public school. This seemed like a wonderful opportunity to continue teaching and offer the children top-notch education. I also loved the idea of Christian training and small classes. Challenges were always motivating to me and this definitely had some big hurdles to get past. The school opened in September, three months after being fired, and we had a most enthusiastic beginning. Future plans and dreams rolled off our tongues as fast as we could visualize them. Heads were in the clouds much of the time, dreaming of what could be ahead. Parents were pleased and enrollment increased.

In December, I decided to get off medication against the doctor's recommendation. Everything was going so well and my self-esteem was growing. I believed I could make it. I believed I could do it on my own.

My world slowly came tumbling down but I kept erroneously thinking I could get a hold of things and make it. I continued to flounder and my hold on reality deteriorated. Everything at school suffered as I struggled to be in control. Finally, after the weeklong ordeal with Satan "putting his spirit in me," I admitted again that I couldn't make it without medication.

By the end of the school year, I knew that this was not where I needed to stay. I felt that I was being used because responsibility was put on me that should have been shared by others. Also, the school did not bring in enough money to pay me a salary. I could not support myself by living solely off unemployment. It was time to reach out in new and different areas. My friends surely felt betrayed, as the school could not continue without my help. My efforts to explain my leaving were entirely inadequate and probably added to their hurt and lack of understanding of the situation. But I knew for sure that I needed to move on when other friends began urging me to do so. They were able to see the problems as clearly as I did.

Not knowing what I would do and still too wounded and scared from my public school experience to be out in the world, I opened a Christian school in my home and taught four boys that year. These boys had special needs and I loved working closely with them and dealing with their unique behavioral and emotional requirements. My financial situation continued to mimic a pauper, as I could not bring myself to ask for more than the parents could afford to pay. But mostly, as I look back on the two years after my dismissal, it seems like I hid out, afraid to be hurt again. Like a dog that has been beaten, I was too frightened to venture out and look beyond the familiar and safe.

I was alone a lot and had time and reason to seek God out and spend entire evenings and weekends with Him. Aloneness can be the quickest path to God. As Eugenia Price says, "If there is no one close to hold our hand, we may take God's hand more readily and hold on more tightly." Hard times create a need for God. Adversity forces us to be the best we can be. Whenever I was faced with an adverse problem, I had a decision to make. How would I respond? Would I become bitter, hateful and angry? Or would I become better and turn to God for my answers and direction?

Some deep issues needed to be resolved before I went any further in life. I had to, finally, once and for all decide if I was going to continue to believe that I was worthless and not a good teacher, parent, wife, and child. Was I going to continue to accept the blame and shame of the past that piled higher and higher upon me? Was I willing to continue to live like this? Was I really this terrible person? Did I deserve to lose my job or were there other things at work in that situation? How much longer did I want to live face down in the dirt believing I deserved to stay there? What did God's Word have to say about this? Did God say He expected me to do penance and make amends for my past mistakes forever? Was I going to continue to let other people's opinions determine my happiness and the way I saw myself? Did I have any other choices available to me? Did I like being a negative person that could not trust other people? Could I do something different about my worry, anxiety and fears? Was God really Who He said He was? I came to my conclusion. I could not continue living like this. I was too miserable.

Public school doors seemed shut for me and private schools could not provide enough financially. Since I was so hesitant about being vulnerable again in the outside world, I was more willing to wait on the Lord. At the same time, the severe lack of money pushed and prodded me to find a teaching position. Interviews were so difficult. I feared telling my job history, and being ridden with guilt, it was next to impossible to present myself in a positive and confident manner. My good qualities were hidden under the wall-to-wall carpets of self-blame and shame. With the coaching of friends, and after practicing what they said to say, I found interviews becoming easier and less stressful.

I was hired by a therapeutic counseling center. My job was to teach adolescents with emotional and behavioral problems. What a challenge and stretching experience! But I knew I had to make it. There was no choice in my mind. I could not be a failure again. I had to prove I was a good teacher. Otherwise, the people who had fired me would be right about who I was as a teacher and a person. Talk about separating the wheat from the chaff and taking out the impurities with fire and intense heat! These kids knew how to do it well! The job was so exhausting and demanding mentally, physically and emotionally that it was all I could do to drag myself to work each day. This job had the potential to either make me or break me.

It forced me to 1. choose what I believed about myself and to 2.

decide my values and 3. determine if I had any self-worth. Did I really deserve respect from others? Would I be able to command it by my self-respectful words and actions? These kids were able to pick on me in ways that I never considered. They were never at a loss to try to upset and anger me. They tested me without mercy to see if I too would leave as their last teacher had. They didn't want me there; they wanted their old teacher back.

One adolescent boy told me that I would never make it as a teacher in this setting. At first I believed what he said was true. Then I determined that I would indeed make it and I would show this little guy that he did not know what he was talking about. The job began hardening me to difficulties, and to what people said about me and to me. I began becoming my own person. It was like being face to face with a man-eating lion. Either you master it, or you die.

In less than a year, I loved my work and loved the adolescents even more. And they loved and respected me. This job seemed perfectly tailored to my needs. Where I was weak, it challenged me. It gave me everything I lacked emotionally. It wasn't easy; but it sure was worth it. I stayed with them for one year. Then another opportunity in the same facility arose to work with troubled elementary aged kids.

When I began working with children, instead of adolescents, I found the most nurturing and caring environment I'd ever known. The supervisors and staff treated me with profound respect and admiration. Unconditional love and acceptance was overwhelming at times. Accepting me with all my quirks and mistakes was natural and normal. With this position, I came to love myself just the way I am. I don't mind making mistakes anymore. They're simply an opportunity to learn. I don't demand perfection of myself any more; I'm glad to be who I am. Self-confident and self-respectful now describes me. I was not able to give to others what they needed until I first gave to myself what I needed. A person can only give away what they own. And a person can only lead where they have been.

God has taken what I perceived to be my shameful weaknesses and has changed them to become admirable strengths. Because of my history, I have insight to people and emotional problems that many do not have. I am able to understand why people do certain things and why it is so hard to change. Much of my life, my sensitivity was seen as a problem. Now I am able to use that sensitive spirit to understand others' needs and put myself in their shoes. It is easy for me to have compassion. My experiences have given me understanding and to know how to help. My illness with its many problems has been my greatest teacher and my greatest asset in being able to help others. People who are hurting, especially children, are my soft spot because I have hurt so much. God has given me freely in so many different ways. I want to give back some of what had been given to me.

"There is no finer sensation in life than that which comes with victory over one's self. It feels good to go fronting into a hard wind, winning against its power; but it feels a thousand times better to go forward to a goal of inward achievement, brushing aside all your old internal enemies as you advance." Vash Young

Affirmations from God's Word

Enter into peace and in freedom from all the distresses that are experienced as the result of sin. *Luke 7:50*

...He is the rewarder of those who earnestly and diligently seek Him out. *Hebrews 11:6*

He who practices truth - who does what is right - comes out into the light; so that his works may be plainly shown to be what they are, wrought with God - divinely prompted, done with God's help, in dependence upon Him. *John 3:21*

I will cry to God Most High, Who performs on my behalf and rewards me (Who brings to pass His purposes for me and surely completes them)! *Psalm 57:2*

...one thing I do and it is my one aspiration: forgetting what lies behind and straining forward to what lies ahead. *Philippians 3:13*

Only let us hold true to what we have already attained and walk and order our lives by that. *Philippians 3:16*

Though now for a little while you may be distressed by trials and suffer temptations, so that the genuineness of your faith may be tested, your faith which is infinitely more precious than the perishable gold which is tested and purified by fire. This proving of your faith is intended to redound to your praise and glory and honor when Jesus Christ, the Messiah, the Anointed One is revealed. *Peter 1:6,7*

Blows that wound cleanse away evil, and strokes for correction reach to the innermost parts. *Proverbs 20:30*

He is always striving for you earnestly in His prayers, pleading that you may - as persons of ripe character and clear conviction - stand firm and mature in spiritual growth, convinced and fully assured in everything willed by God. *Colossians 4:12*

Let us then fearlessly and confidently and boldly draw near to the throne of grace - the throne of God's unmerited favor to us sinners; that we may receive mercy for our failures and find grace to help in good time for every need - appropriate help and well-timed help, coming just when we need it. *Hebrews 4:16*

For I consider that the sufferings of this present time (this present life) are not worth being compared with the glory that is about to be revealed to us and in us and for us, and conferred on us! *Romans 8:18*

And He will establish you to the end - keep you steadfast, give you strength, and guarantee your vindication, that is, be your warrant against all accusation or indictment - so that you will be guiltless and irreproachable in the day of our Lord Jesus Christ, the Messiah. God is faithful - reliable, trustworthy and therefore ever true to His promise, and He can be depended upon; by Him you were called in to companionship and participation with His Son, Jesus Christ our Lord. *I Corinthians 1:9.*

Casting the whole of your care - all your anxieties, all your worries, all your concerns, once and for all - on Him; for He cares for you affectionately, and cares about you watchfully. *I Peter 5:7*

We are assured and know that (God being a partner in their labor), all things work together and are (fitting into a plan) for good to those who love God and are called according to His design and purpose. *Romans 8:28*

For God did not send the Son into the world in order to judge - to reject, to condemn, to pass sentence on, - the world; but that it might find salvation and be made safe and sound through Him. *John 3:17*

Those whom I dearly and tenderly love, I tell their faults and convict and convince and reprove and chasten and I discipline and instruct them. So be enthusiastic and in earnest and burning with zeal and repent and change your mind and attitude. *Revelation 3:19*

And I will restore or replace for you the years that the locust has eaten. *Joel 2:25*

I will return to My place on high until they acknowledge their offense and feel their guilt and seek My face; in their affliction and distress they will seek, inquire for, and require Me earnestly, saying, Come and let us return to the Lord, for He has torn so that He may heal us; He has stricken so that He may bind us up. *Hosea 5:15-6:1*

Reflective Reassurance

God takes us one step at a time toward health when He knows we are ready. He never expects us to do something He has not prepared us to do. He is always motivated by love and compassion for us.

Chapter 17
Learning to Cope Is What It's All About.
More strategies for creating hope, health and happiness

My motivation for change was coming from within me, the only source that produces the courage and the tenacity to do the hard things involved in turning one's life around. I do not have the power to change another person, only myself. Dr. Mike Murdock, founder of Wisdom Keys, reminds us, "When you want something you've never had before, you have to do something you've never done before." If you want to understand miracles, you must become a miracle.

It was so tempting at times for me to go back to the "old country" as a slave to perfectionism and in bondage to fear and depression. Sometimes I thought going back would be better for it seemed easier than what I had to do. Many times I have chosen not to do anything about my negative thoughts or fears even though I knew what to do to help myself. However, I have learned that I cannot look back to the "old country" - the way of sickness. I must go on to the Promised Land. For their are two plans for my life - Satan's plan and God's plan. I had to choose whom I wanted to follow.

In John 5:2-8 is this story: Now there is in Jerusalem a pool near the Sheep Gate. This pool in the Hebrew is called Bethesda, having five porches (alcoves, colonnades, doorways). In these lay a great number of sick folk - some blind, some crippled, and some paralyzed (shriveled up) - waiting for the bubbling up of the water. For an angel of the Lord went down at appointed seasons into the pool and moved and stirred up the water; whoever then first, after the stirring up of the water, stepped in was cured of whatever disease with which he was afflicted. There was a certain man there who had suffered with a deep-seated and lingering disorder for thirty-eight years. When Jesus noticed him lying there helpless, knowing that he had already been a long time in that condition, He said to him, Do you want to become well? Are you really in earnest about getting well? The invalid answered, Sir, I have nobody when the water is moving to put me into the pool; but while I am trying to come into it myself, somebody else steps down ahead of me. Jesus said to him, Get up! Pick up your bed (sleeping pad) and walk!...

I had to ask myself those two questions. Did I want to become well? Was I really in earnest about getting well? Was I really in earnest about making changes in my life? For in a very real sense I was crippled, blind, paralyzed and shriveled up. Anger, fear, stubbornness, pride, self-centeredness and hate were debilitating and deadly. They became malignancies that suffocated and choked out the most precious things in my life. They poisoned relationships between parent and child, husband and wife, and friends. They destroyed my marriage, took away my job, self-esteem and confidence and the ability to love and trust. They almost destroyed me and everything and one I held dear.

We need Someone to unravel the tangled mess of our lives. I picture Jesus with the huge pile of my tangled, knotted and matted yarn of my life on His lap. He is ever so patiently and tenderly unraveling it, and taking out each knot, thorn and sticker. When we try to untangle something we sometimes have to start all over in a different way. Or maybe we can't figure it out and we just cut it or give up. God never has to go back and redo. He knows perfectly what to do first and then what to do next. And He never gives up. It's never too hard or too tiring or too frustrating for Him. He's the Perfect Unraveler of anything that we have made a mess of or that is messed up in our life. As the matted mess of my life has continued to be unraveled, God is making, as He has promised, a finished product that will be one of beauty and usefulness.

When we finally answer yes to the questions, Do you want to become well? and Are you really in earnest about getting well; then we must.... Get up and walk! We must start doing the things we need to do to make our life different. We must...Get up and walk! And make the changes we need to make.

We must concentrate on our strengths rather than our weaknesses and what we cannot do. Our answers will not be found in our problems; but rather, in the things we are doing when we are problem-free. There are times, maybe only brief, when we do not hear voices, when we are not fearful and when we are not hiding in bed. Taking a close look at what is happening then can be the key to having longer problem-free periods and making continued progress. We need to examine what we are doing and who we are with when occupied with thoughts and activities that seem to encourage the best in us. Then we must repeat those thoughts and activities again and again to strengthen and enlarge the positive and healthy spirit within us.

It was so exciting for me to reread the parable of the talents and see clearly, what was being rewarded. I have spent a large part of my life trying to fix my weaknesses and amend for my shortcomings. Dwelling on what was wrong with me and how I could improve was my focus. Read again with me the parable of the talents in Matthew 25:14-21; 24-25. For it is like a man who was about to take a long journey and he called his servants together and entrusted them with his property. To one he gave five talents (probably about $5,000), to another two, to another one - to each in proportion to his own personal ability. Then he departed and left the country. He who had received the five talents went at once and traded with them, and he gained five talents more. And likewise he who had received the two talents - he also gained two talents more. But he who had received the one talent went and dug a hole in the ground and hid his master's money. Now after a long time the master of those servants returned and settled accounts with them. And he who had received the five talents came and brought him five more, saying, Master, you entrusted to me five talents; see, here I have gained five talents more. His master said to him, Well done, you upright (honorable, admirable) and faithful servant! You have been faithful and trustworthy over a little; I will put you in charge of much. Enter into and share the joy (the delight, the blessedness) which your master enjoys…He who had received one talent also came forward, saying, Master, I knew you to be a harsh and hard man, reaping where you did not sow, and gathering where you had not winnowed (the grain). So I was afraid, and I went and hid your talent in the ground. Here you have what is your own."

This person was rewarded for developing and increasing what he had been given in the way of a gift. He was given even more as he used his assets in activities that produced more abundance. We cannot continue to live in fear and dread and bury our assets so deeply that we forget or never realize what we have been given. At every stage and turn in our life, we are given what we need to do well. God will be sure to give when He knows we are ready to receive. The successes of the past, no matter how small, prepare us to succeed even more in other areas. As we begin to succeed, our positive and healthy spirit grows stronger and larger. It becomes easier to deal with our problems and we are able to understand and use truth in our lives. Little by little, the truth begins to free our mind, our body and our heart from all distresses. What had been taken from me ruled my life and spirit. When I determined to focus on my strengths and what I had been given, I began to heal and prosper. What is important is what we've been given.

How do we begin when we have been beaten down for so long? The battle is so hard and it seems to go on and on without relief. We begin small and we begin with the help of someone we trust. There is usually someone we know whom we admire greatly and want to be like. I remember saying about someone I knew, "I want what she's got. I want to know what she knows." She, along with other Christian women in my life, have been my role models and mentors. Having a role model is like having a goal in mind that you want to attain. You aspire to be like this person by watching them and "picking their brain." Find out how they handle problems and listen to what they tell you about yourself. Be open to new ideas and different ways of doing things. Listen carefully and ask questions when you do not understand. Continue to ask until you get it. These may be your answers to finding hope and new direction for your life.

I have learned that praising God for Who He is and what He has done in my life is the most effective way to calm my fears and be at peace. It is much easier to trust God when I recount all the ways He has been there for me. I ask Him to remind me how He made my dark spirits flee and how He has turned my children's hearts back to me in love. When I list His attributes and praise His qualities, I am able to rest in His strength and power. My thoughts are no longer on me but on the magnificent God of the universe, Who is capable in every way.

Managing stress is of critical concern for all areas of our health. Many times the stress level of our life at home and work and in our relationships is the best indicator of whether to expect problems and eventual relapse or continued well being. We need to know what is creating the stress. Consider and study thoughtfully and prayerfully the mistaken beliefs that are fueling stress. This will enable us to locate and address the root of the stress. Stress management effectiveness can be increased with aerobic exercise, muscular relaxation techniques, massage therapy, time management, anger management, parenting skills, communication skills and assertiveness training. Sometimes we find that we have been managing our stress inappropriately through drugs, alcohol or overeating.

Physical exercise, adequate sleep and good nutrition need to be a way of life for everyone, especially those who struggle emotionally. Chemicals in the brain are responsible for mood and thought processes. They are affected positively or negatively by our diet, sleep and exercise habits. Consider this way of life to be something you must do in order to maintain emotional well being. Strive to find comfort in your relationship with God rather than food or drink. Start every morning by turning your desires to Him, pledging to run to Him first when troubled, anxious or bored. The more we rely on Him, the less we will need other means of support for our solace.

Learn to take action. Anxiety and worry is many times a substitute for action. Doing something, no matter how small to help ourselves, energizes and empowers us to do even more. Washing the dishes, pulling weeds, anything no matter how mundane, can help give us the edge we need to not become buried in what troubles us.

Giving God all of my Sunday is a way of taking care of myself. When Sunday is set aside for rest from work and I fill it with time with God and His Word, I find that I am renewed, refreshed and strengthened. Attending church and Bible study regularly introduces me to truth and helps it to penetrate my way of thinking. I find answers to my problems as I get to know God better and better. Wisdom and truth become my friends; and I am prepared to meet the challenges of the week with confidence and praise rather than fear and impotence.

A Bible study guide can be an excellent way to find direction and focus in applying God's Word to our life situation. There are studies available on each book of the Bible, on specific persons in the Bible and on selected topics such as forgiveness, God's character or the reasons we have no joy. As you visit various Christian book stores, you will no doubt find studies that will help you grow and mature in emotional and spiritual health.

Writing our life story or parts of it is an excellent way to see how everything fits together for good. We can let go of hard things as we write, edit, read and reread what we have written. The more we write and read about the same situations, the more desensitized to the trauma we become. It is like telling someone the same story over and over in detail until it no longer evokes the same depth of emotion and can be spoken of more objectively. Writing enables us to work out problems in our minds and see people and happenings in a new perspective. It has proved to be a major catalyst in my journey to wholeness.

Learn to take time to think rather than just automatically react. Our greatest wealth is in having the freedom to choose. We can choose our actions and our responses. We can be who we desire to be and not just the person we think we have to be or always have been. We will find that the way people treat us is pretty much the way we ask to be treated. It takes courage and determination to do and think differently; but it is possible for all who pursue it without giving up.

Look back to the past only to learn from it. Anything more is only a hindrance at best. We are stuck as long as we stay in the past of the "old country". We can't change the past, but we can let it go and move on in newfound wisdom and compassion for others and ourselves.

When we were physically born, we had no past. When we are spiritually born, we no longer have a past either. Old things are passed away and all things have become new. God's complete forgiveness makes us white as snow. We have a new Father, a new future and a new inheritance.

When we are tempted to go back to the "old country," we must ask ourselves what will be stolen from us and what will be destroyed. We must also ask ourself what lies Satan is asking us to believe. What will we look like if we continue to give in again and again to this temptation? We must search for healthy ways to meet our needs.

When others have wronged us or not met our needs, we may spend years trying to get that person to do the things we missed. Expecting someone to give something they do not have within themselves to give causes much frustration and disappointment for us. After wasting much time being angry with my parents for not saying and doing what I thought they should, I decided to be content and enjoy whatever legitimate source could meet my needs. I stopped demanding that my parents be something they were not. I strive to accept them now as they are. My needs for unconditional love and feeling special have been met through my sisters and friends and this continues to be more than good enough.

The greater our feelings of guilt, the greater our inclination to place blame on others or ourselves. Blame only produces punishment and a shutting out of pleasure and joy. Condemnation and criticalness stamp out enthusiasm and love of life. Faultfinding is never motivating and does not create a yearning to excel. It takes away the good in us. Blaming helps to destroy dreams and squelch hopes. It leaves us empty, useless and powerless. Learn to look for what is right and can be praised in people and situations. In everything, there is some good. Seek to find it.

The armor of a soldier is all on his front as he marches into battle. As long as we face the enemy with our armor of the truth of God's Word, faith and righteousness, we are protected and prevail. When we turn away from these, we are left vulnerable and unprotected. Set aside a quiet time each day to meditate on Scripture, maybe just one verse. Spend time in prayer praising and thanking God daily for all that He does for our benefit.

God has a plan for our life and there is purpose in our pain. He works in us for a greater purpose — to work through us. He is always Lord, whether it be in the good times or the painful times. We are only as close to Him as we choose to be. It is our responsibility to come to know God well, for life here is preparing us for life in eternity. But God can only do what we allow Him to do. He will never force Himself on us because His love respects us too much.

From *God Calling*, edited by A. J. Russell, comes the following: "Think how tenderly I respect the right of each individual soul. Never forcing upon it My Help, My Salvation. Perhaps in all My suffering for humanity that is the hardest, the restraint of the Divine Impatience and longing to help, until the call of the soul gives Me My right to act. Think of Love shown in this. Comfort My waiting, loving, longing Heart by claiming My Help, Guidance and Miracle-working Power."

Jesus said that the very hairs of our head are all numbered (Luke 12:7). How closely God attends to us and watches every aspect of our being! To know the number of the hairs on our head is amazing, in and of itself. But consider that the number is always changing. Every time we wash our hair, brush it, run our fingers through it, or toss and turn in our sleep, the number changes. Hairs just fall out on their own for no apparent reason while new ones come in without our knowing. But, God always knows the number of our hairs! There is no way that man could accomplish such a feat. God can never take His eye off of us for if He did, He would miss a falling hair.

God knows everything about us at every moment. He carefully attends to us and gives us His strict attention. He is waiting for each one of us to turn to Him and ask for His help. Do not delay any longer. God yearns to love us, give us mercy and freedom from all the distresses caused by the sin in our life. God will not disappoint us or let us down in any way. He turns no one away. In Getting through the Night, by Eugenia Price, she attributes the following to God:

> *All which I took from thee*
> *I did but take, not for thy harms,*
> *but just that thou might'st seek it in My arms.*

Go forth! And be healthy and happy!

Affirmations From God's Word

You have turned my mourning into dancing for me; You have put off my sackcloth and girded me with gladness. To the end that my tongue and my heart and everything glorious within me may sing praises to You and not be silent, O Lord my God, I will give thanks to You forever. *Psalm 30:11,12*

I waited patiently and expectantly for the Lord; and He inclined to me and heard my cry. He drew me up out of a terrible pit (a pit of tumult and of destruction) out of the miry clay (froth and slime), and set my feet upon a rock, steadying my steps and establishing my goings. And He has put a new song in my mouth, a song of praise to our God. *Psalm 40:1-6*